RESTRUCTURING

The key to effective school management

Cyril Poster

Edited by Sonia Blandford
and John Welton

London and New York

First published 1999
by Routledge
11 New Fetter Lane, London EC4P 4EE

Simultaneously published in the USA and Canada
by Routledge
29 West 35th Street, New York, NY 10001

Routledge is an imprint of the Taylor & Francis Group

© 1999 Cyril Poster; edited by Sonia Blandford and John Welton

Typeset in Garamond by
The Florence Group, Stoodleigh, Devon

Printed and bound in Great Britain by
MPG Books Ltd, Bodmin

British Library Cataloging in Publication Data
A catalogue record for this book is available from the
British Library

Library of Congress Cataloging in Publication Data
Poster, C. D.
Restructuring: the key to effective school management/
Cyril Poster; edited by Sonia Blandford and John Welton
Includes bibliographical references.
1. School management and organization – Great Britain – Case
studies.   2. School improvement programs – Great Britain –
Case studies.   3. Education change – Great Britain – Case studies.
I. Blandford, Sonia.   II. Welton, John.   III. Title.
IV. Title: Key to effective school management.
LB2900.5.P67 1999
371.2'00941–dc21   98–37419

ISBN 0 415 20217 5 (hbk)
ISBN 0 415 20218 3 (pbk)

CONTENTS

CONTENTS

ILLUSTRATIONS

Figures

Tables

FOREWORD

Cyril completed the research for his doctorate at Oxford Brookes University and for this book just days before his death in September 1997. Cyril was a pioneer and visionary of comprehensive education and one of the most distinguished headteachers of his generation. His experience as the principal of newly established comprehensive schools was recognised in his appointment from 1984–1986 as Senior Research Fellow and Deputy Director of the National Development Centre for School Management Training at University of Bristol School of Education. Cyril was a prolific writer and made an outstanding contribution to the study and practice of school management as editor of the Routledge Educational Management series.

In his PhD thesis, Cyril acknowledged the help which he had received from many people. From his university supervisors, Peter Earley and myself and, in particular, Dr Shirley Hord from Texas. Cyril first met Dr Hord at an ISIP conference in 1983, and in 1984 she introduced him to the Concerns-based Adoption Model (CBAM) in an intensive five-day personal tuition programme. Cyril greatly valued the continued contact. He remembered Dr Hord as a valued critic and selective supplier of North American literature on restructuring not readily available in the UK.

Cyril also acknowledged the tolerance of the busy headteachers and staff of the five schools involved in his research, without which the case study chapters would have been difficult to complete.

In his thesis Cyril paid tribute to the support which he had received from his wife Doreen with whom he had written and published during their long marriage. He wrote:

> My wife has been patience personified. Writing, whether of books or a thesis, can become a compulsion: the worry is that the idea or phrase may never be recaptured once it is allowed to escape. Meals and periods of rest and recreation are, however, important and she has been a constant reminder that there are other things in life besides my computer. . . .

Sonia Blandford and I feel that our lives have been enriched by our friendship with Cyril and Doreen and that we are privileged to have been invited to complete the editing of his final research for publication. We thank Doreen for her confidence in us and for her support in the final editorial process. We also thank Helen James for her extensive and meticulous help in the process of adapting the thesis to book form.

Cyril's life's work was concerned with the topic of this book: restructuring education. He provided an exemplar in the way he supported hard-pressed teachers and others concerned with improving the conditions in which children learn. His practical work as a headteacher and his work in consultancy and as a writer encouraged teachers and school managers with whom he had contact to work to the highest possible professional standards. His best memorial will be the continuation of this work.

John Welton

ACKNOWLEDGEMENTS

The views expressed in this book are those of the author, Cyril Poster, and are represented to the best of the editors' ability. The editors are grateful to all participating schools for their permission to be cited in the text.

ABBREVIATIONS

ACAS	Advisory, Conciliation and Arbitration Service
AERA	American Education Research Association
BEMAS	British Educational Management and Administration Society
BSI	British Standards Institution
CBAM	Concerns-based Adoption Model
CIPFA	Chartered Institute of Public Finance and Accountancy
COSMOS	Committee on the Organisation, Staffing and Management of Schools
CSE	Certificate of Secondary Education
CTCs	City technology colleges
DES	Department of Education and Science
DfEE	Department for Education and Employment
DVE	Diploma in Vocational Education
FICSI	Foundation for International Collaboration on School Improvement
GCE	General Certificate of Education
GCSE	General Certificate of Secondary Education
GM	Grant maintained
GNVQ	General National Vocational Qualification
GRASP	Getting Results and Solving Problems
HEADLAMP	Headteacher Leadership and Management Programme
HMI	Her Majesty's Inspectorate
ICSEI	International Congress for School Effectiveness and Improvement
IIP	Investors in People
INSET	in-service training
ISIP	International School Improvement Project
KS 1/2/4	Key Stage 1/2/4
LEAs	local education authorities
LFM	local financial management
LMS	local management of schools
LoU	Levels of Use

MCI	Management Charter Initiative
NAHT	National Association of Head Teachers
NDC	National Development Centre for School Management Training
NEAC	National Education Assessment Centre
NNEB	National Nursery Education Board
NQT	newly qualified teacher
OECD	Organisation for Economic Cooperation and Development
OFSTED	Office for Standards in Education
OTTO	one-term training opportunities
PGCE	Postgraduate Certificate in Education
PTA	Parent–Teachers' Association
QA	quality assurance
QC	quality control
RSA	Royal Society of Arts
SAT	Standard Attainment Tests
SBM	school-based management
SEN	special educational needs
SMAs	school meals assistants
SoC	Stages of Concern
SWOT	strengths, weaknesses, opportunities, threats
TES	*Times Educational Supplement*
TQM	total quality management

INTRODUCTION
Why restructuring?

Restructuring is a concept that, in relation to school improvement and school effectiveness, has increasing currency in the United States. It may be that some of the misconceptions about and abuses of the concept have deterred British educationalists from giving restructuring the attention that it deserves. In a number of American states or districts within states restructuring has been made mandatory. This is clearly putting the cart before the horse, since restructuring is a process that facilitates change, and it is only when decisions have been taken on what changes would best advance the learning in a school that restructuring is to be brought into the equation.

Again, in the USA, as in several Australian states and Canadian provinces, restructuring is often equated with school-based management (SBM). As with local management of schools (LMS) in England and Wales, the benefits of SBM are often obscured by the high degree of centralised control over what are ostensibly decentralised procedures.

The contribution that restructuring makes to school improvement and effectiveness meets this criticism. Central to the theory and practice of restructuring is the notion that change must be holistic: that any change in one area of management will inevitably affect all aspects of the school's management. For example, putting resources such as time into one development will almost inevitably take away resources from other aspects of the running of the school, and particularly when school staff judge themselves to be already at full stretch. Unless there is a clear and coherent plan for development over a period of time and, subject to stringent monitoring and evaluation, of a kind consistent with the developmental aims of that school, then effective change will be inhibited.

Yet restructuring is far more than a means of delivering change. Its key exponents posit that schools need to have in place not only the 'core technology of teaching' (Elmore *et al.* 1990) but two variables additional to these 'central variables' (Conley 1993). These Conley describes as the *enabling* and *supporting* variables, such as:

1

- school–community relations
- school governance
- working relationships
- the learning environment.

All three variables are there not simply to be called upon to facilitate a development that the school may wish to introduce, but are intrinsic to the management of the school, its maintenance of stability as well as its promotion of change.

It is important that the research leading to the publication of this book should validate the importance of schools, and those responsible for supporting them, evaluating their outcomes over the full range of their activities, actual and potential, as is required in restructuring. To accomplish this, the first two chapters consider the extensive developments in school organisation and management over four post-war decades; the influence on those changes, in the late 1970s and the 1980s in particular, of the growing body of management literature; and the growth of an international perspective on what makes an effective school.

Chapter 1 begins with the mid-1950s, a time when organisational issues were pre-eminent in the minds of those involved in the introduction of comprehensive education in England and Wales. The traditional hierarchical organisation of decision making existed – in comprehensive schools no less than in primary, secondary modern and grammar schools – largely because there were no models within the profession for any other style. Few, if any, headteachers had analysed their role. Had they done so, they might have perceived that it had two inter-related dimensions: the instrumental and the expressive, as Musgrave (1968) was to point out. For them, certainly until the closing years of the 1960s, the instrumental dimension, dealing with curricular and organisational issues, was all-important for the success of these new schools, secondary modern and all-ability alike.

A significant impetus to managerial change came about in the years following the publication of the Newsom Report (1963) and the Plowden Report (1967), both of which promoted the growth of parental involvement; and the following decade saw the evolution in many schools of enhanced roles for pastoral staff. The change was both organisational and managerial; the needs of parents for discussion with tutors on both academic progress and behavioural matters could be accomplished only through a decentralisation of responsibility accompanied, it was soon to become obvious, by in-service training in interpersonal skills.

The 1970s witnessed the burgeoning of a fundamental change of attitude by some experienced headteachers, particularly those in comprehensive schools. There was a growing interest in the common ground between management theory and practice in the workplace and in the school. Key writers, for example Drucker (1970, 1974) on effective management and

Weick (1976) on school organisations as loose-coupled systems, were particularly influential on those headteachers, still very much a minority, who were exploring ideas of management, including those from outside the education system, that might contribute to the improved running of schools, leading to an evaluation of schools' managerial systems.

In the early years of the 1980s, government provided the means for a continuing funding policy for in-service education, within which training to improve the management of schools has been a recurrent heading. No less important was the introduction of five staff training days into the school calendar, enabling a school to identify and meet its own development needs, internally or through consultancy. Appraisal was introduced as a means of evaluating staff development and in-service training needs, and the requirement on schools to produce a three-year rolling school development plan added an important dimension to the internal management of all schools, primary as well as secondary. The mid-1980s will probably be regarded by educational historians as the period during which effective decentralisation of power and authority to local education authorities peaked.

There were now to be a number of enactments, in particular the Education (No. 2) Act (DES 1986a) and the Education Reform Act (DES 1988), of the utmost significance to school management in England and Wales. Radical changes in the governance of schools, and the introduction of local financial management and local management of schools, though the training and support that governors and headteachers needed if they were to implement them effectively were lacking, were broadly beneficial and in line with the intent of decentralisation. The introduction of the National Curriculum, the creation of a new and far less 'user-friendly' form of school inspection conducted by the Office for Standards in Education (OFSTED), and the publication of league tables of Key Stage and external examination results, were all centrally imposed and part of a significant shift to a model of school management necessarily much influenced by powerful agencies created by government. The pace and scope of change were such that, if schools were to cope effectively, they would have to reconsider their management structures, styles and practices. Restructuring offers a means whereby schools can establish and maintain control of external change without surrendering their ability to respond to local needs and their own initiatives.

Chapter 2 outlines the origins and development of the school-improvement project and the school-effectiveness movement, the former promoted by OECD funding. In a number of west European countries and in the USA there has been sustained interest in these two developments, and recently there has been an important attempt to synthesise them (Reynolds *et al.* 1996).

Two fields of research that contributed to the monitoring of school effectiveness, the one concerned with competences (Earley 1992, 1993), the other with quality (West-Burnham 1992), influenced monitoring and evaluation in some schools, but involved time-consuming processes that, at a time when schools were coming under intense pressure, inhibited their wider adoption. A growing body of literature on the concept of leadership was beginning to influence those schools seeking to become more effective. It is one of the purposes of this book to assess the relationship between the school-improvement and school-effectiveness movements, on the one hand, and restructuring, on the other.

Chapter 3 sets out the evolution, principles and processes of restructuring, the model on which was based the empirical research, presented in Chapters 5–9, into the case study schools. Its importance is summed up by Hord (1992: 89):

> Restructuring is a new way of thinking about educational reform. Restructuring is, importantly, stimulated by highly challenging outcomes for students. . . . These outcomes will require a holistic approach, engaging the entire system.

The author set out to test the hypothesis that effective primary and secondary schools have been developing managerial strategies which have much in common with restructuring.

Chapter 4 therefore proposes the research model which is to be applied to five case studies. The main features of the methodology were the gathering of data through in-depth interview and through an extensive study of school documentation. Headteacher interviews were conducted on two days separated by ample time for the author to analyse the school's published literature – both that for parents and the community and that for school and staff development. OFSTED inspections of all but one of the five schools took place either during or after the completion of the case studies, and the findings were not therefore available as data.

Teachers were interviewed using the Stages of Concern (SoC) element of the Concerns-Based Adoption Model (CBAM), described in detail in Chapter 5. Since the first stage of the research was to ascertain that these were indeed effective schools, a checklist for this phase of the research made use of the school-effectiveness criteria evolved by Mortimore (1993) and used extensively in the National Commission on Education studies, *Learning to Succeed* (1993) and *Success Against the Odds* (1996).

Chapters 5–9 contain the case studies of five schools, all at different stages of development, that nevertheless gave promise of providing evidence of a holistic approach in their management strategies. Since there was no available data-bank of effective schools, the choice of schools was made by the researcher based on his knowledge of the school, or the headteacher, or both. In order to provide a common basis for evaluation of the data, the Mortimore school-effectiveness criteria were used as the framework for the summary in each of these five chapters.

Given that these schools then proved to be, on the basis of Mortimore's criteria, effective, the next step was to determine how far they might, individually and collectively, reasonably be described as 'restructuring schools'. For Chapter 10, an analytical model was used that derives from the work of one of the early writers on restructuring (Corbett 1990). There were two reasons for this choice rather than the central, enabling and supporting variables of Conley's 'road map'. The first was that, while the relationship between Corbett's initial concept and Conley's extensive development of it is clear, the detailed commentary on these variables contained in Chapter 3 might be thought to colour the objectivity required for assessing the standing of these schools. The second and perhaps more cogent reason was that, in the period between the publication of Corbett's paper in 1990 and Conley's book in 1993, the researcher had initiated and trialed in his work as an education consultant an analytical model (Figure 10.1) based on Corbett's four elements of roles, responsibilities, rules and results, a model directed particularly to the organisational and managerial issues applicable to restructuring in England and Wales.

Chapter 11 looks at the lessons which may be learnt from the case studies and their analysis in terms of the restructuring criteria. It then examines the ways in which restructuring is able to further the development of school effectiveness in England and Wales. It looks at both the potentialities and the constraints, including the role of the governing body and the change agents, within and without the school, that can contribute to the restructuring process. It reaffirms the need for considering restructuring not as a panacea but as a continuous process, one that routinely reviews and evaluates all aspects of the school's organisation and management.

1

ORGANISATION AND MANAGEMENT IN POST-WAR SCHOOLS

Introduction

This chapter examines the major changes in educational practice from the mid-1950s to the mid-1980s. Without an understanding of the nature of organisation and management practices in schools in this period, it is unlikely that the impact of the school-improvement and school-effectiveness movements (see Chapter 2) and the concept of restructuring which they generated will be understood.

Grammar schools and early comprehensives

The grammar school attended by the author provided what would then have been regarded as a good education, albeit one concerned with stasis, not change. The curriculum led inexorably, year by year, to the examination goals essential to future academic careers. Those pupils deemed 'not of examination calibre' disappeared quietly at the end of a school year.

The role of parents was strictly circumscribed. They received and countersigned the termly report on which appeared our rank order in class, examination marks and brief phrases of the order of 'satisfactory' and, more frequently, 'can do better'. Speech Day and the annual school play or orchestral concert were the sole occasions when parents set foot in the school, unless sent for by the headteachers.

The headteacher's professional leadership of his or her staff was directed mainly to maintaining and increasing the prestige of the school. All else followed from that. The only explicit aspect of school administration appears to have been organisational and delegated to the senior master or mistress: absence cover, room changes, examination arrangements, the detention list, as announced at the end of morning assembly or by notes to the classroom. The published accounts of pre-war grammar and public schools, for example in the two symposia published in 1936 and entitled *The Headmaster Speaks* and *The Headmistress Speaks* – long out of print but cited by Baron (1968: 1–2) – suggest that there is nothing exceptional in this account. The influence of Thomas Arnold of Rugby was pervasive. 'His conception of headship was inherited and realised by devoted disciples from his staff' (Rée 1968: 112). His son Matthew was responsible, through his position in the newly established corps of HMI, for translating the ethos of the public school to the new state-subsidised grammar schools by the appointment of many headteachers cast in the Arnold mould.

Almost all headteachers and senior staff of the 350 or so comprehensive schools that had opened in the two decades to 1965 (Benn and Simon 1972: 336) had been educated in grammar schools and would have had their entire teaching experience in grammar schools. The route to seniority from those with comprehensive experience was, before the rapid expansion that followed *Circular 10/65* (DES 1965), understandably rare.

Few colleges and university departments as yet played any part in preparing their education students for the experience of working in comprehensive schools. In 1965 the National Union of Students surveyed the three-year secondary course in colleges of education and discovered that fewer than one-third of final-year students had even visited a comprehensive school, let alone been prepared for the possibility of teaching in one.

College and university lecturers rarely had first-hand knowledge of comprehensive schools. Some were, by political conviction, advocates of comprehensive education; others were, almost certainly, indifferent to and unaware of the demands that this educational and social revolution was already beginning to make; and there were a few highly vocal critics. For example, Cox and Dyson (1969) were beginning what was to be a lengthy and often vituperative rearguard action against what they saw as egalitarianism, social engineering and the destruction of a tried and tested educational system.

Organisation in the early comprehensives

The cornerstone of social organisation in the first two decades of comprehensive schooling was undoubtedly the 'house' system, taken over from the grammar schools, which in their turn had adopted it from the public schools. For the latter the houses were, of course, the places of residence of boarders, a subset of the school, concerning themselves with all that lay outside the academic role of the institution, and replicating in their strata of staff, house captain and prefects, and house members the pyramidal structure of the school itself. The responsibilities of the housemaster during term, as both carer and disciplinarian, were of paramount importance.

The adoption of the house system by the grammar school sought to achieve parity with the public school, but this was largely symbolic. Heads of house, house captains and house prefects had limited powers compared with their public school counterparts; discipline was almost invariably the responsibility of the form master/mistress or subject teacher, not the concern of the house.

It began to be perceived that, to counter the academic multilateralism of the early comprehensive schools, there was need of a mixed-ability grouping to demonstrate the school's concern for all its pupils. This the house structure appeared initially to offer. However, by 1968, as the research by Benn and Simon (1972: 219) on the internal organisation of British comprehensive schools demonstrates, the house system was in decline in favour of a year or house–year system.

The school as an organisation

The use within educational circles of the term 'organisation' was confined largely to that of means to an end: the headteacher could no longer be personally involved in the control of the manifold activities of the large and complex school.

In the organisational structure of most schools there were major inequalities in what is now regarded as a peer group. The curriculum leaders were regarded as having higher status than those with pastoral responsibility. There is no doubt that this caused organisational stress. Yet was there any alternative to an organisational structure that was potentially both divisive and dysfunctional?

The development of organisational theory and practice

There was a growing awareness among senior staff, particularly those who had advanced their knowledge through higher degrees or diplomas, that schools would be more effective if they took account of organisational theory, particularly as it was being applied to schools by leading thinkers such as Musgrave:

> For an organisation to reach its goal, coordination is essential and therefore to anyone analysing organisations a major emphasis must be on the problem of who has power and how it is used. Under contemporary conditions a very common mode of coordinating activity and regulating power is to establish a bureaucracy. For sociologists this term has a definite meaning. *It refers to a hierarchy of positions each of which is governed by known rules and to which incumbents are recruited in a more or less regulated way.* By this very rational method the organisation is able to continue for the purpose for which it was set up despite changes in its personnel.
>
> (Musgrave 1968: 7)

Nevertheless many headteachers continued to prize their autonomy and were not readily affected by what they regarded as influences from outside the profession. Few headteachers had taken it upon themselves to analyse their role. Musgrave follows Etzioni (1964) in pointing out that their role has two dimensions: the instrumental and the expressive. The former includes 'decisions relating to the curriculum, the timetable, external examinations and streaming' (1968: 42).

Some headteachers would, at this point in the development of comprehensive education, have considered the adoption of the expressive role an indication that they were too near the permissive end of the spectrum. For them the key decisions lay in the instrumental dimension. There was now in most comprehensive schools a wide range of ways of structuring classes in the core subjects: by streaming in some subjects, banding or setting in others. This, not to mention the increasing complexity of the curriculum, with the introduction of subjects or variants of existing subjects, to meet the needs of the full range of ability, was making the construction of the timetable a millstone around the neck of the member of staff responsible, usually the curriculum deputy headteacher.

It was clear that a far more scientific–mathematical approach to the implications for timetabling of decisions on curriculum and teaching group organisation was needed. In 1967 the DES set up a team of HMI and others called the Committee on the Organisation, Staffing and Management of Schools (COSMOS). The task assigned to the team was

> to mount a quick series of short courses [in management], to consider longer-term solutions of the problem and to collect or create material and devise methods through which new skills might be developed.
>
> (Murray White 1974)

The main objective of the courses was perhaps more limited than had originally been conceived, which was an examination in depth of the use of resources, particularly those of teaching power and time. The team evolved a technique known as curriculum analysis. Using simple analytical tools, a school was now able to create guidelines for the use of non-teaching periods at the various levels of management within the school structure. The greater openness of organisational decision making that this aspect of the COSMOS courses brought about was an early indication of the movement towards the corporate management that evolved over the next two decades.

Leadership style was now becoming a major preoccupation of educational writers and researchers, for example Fiedler (1967), Greenfield (1975), Hoyle (1976), but the extent to which headteachers were influenced to examine the implications of the way they performed is a matter of some doubt. In a significant research project Hughes (1976) studied the responses of headteachers and staff members from a stratified random sample of maintained secondary schools to two role models of headship: the head as chief executive

9

and the head as leading professional. For each role Hughes (ibid.: 51) posited pairs of polarities: an internal and an external sector in the case of the chief executive role, and a relationship between an innovating and traditional dimension for the leading professional role.

For the leading professional role the findings were less easy to anticipate. The two dimensions of innovation and tradition were 'largely independent of each other, rather than antithetical aspects of the head's role' (ibid.: 53). As might be expected there was a significant interpenetration of the two role models.

Nevertheless, while Hughes' research promoted the concept of differential aspects of the headteacher's role, it did not attempt any indication of how she/he might manage them. Maintaining the health of the organisation in the context of changing internal and external circumstances calls for a high level of management skills.

Where might the headteacher look, then, for some overarching concept which would enable the creation of a structure that would both cope with change and be able to maintain organisational health? The answer, some realised, lay in the definition of two 'ideal' types of organisation defined by the sociologists Burns and Stalker (1968):

> [The mechanistic type is] suitable to stable conditions, to a hier-archical management structure in which there is a clear definition of assigned roles, formal and mainly vertical communication, and a built-in system of checks and supervision. In such a system, because the overall strategy is known only at the top, innovation from the grass roots is unlikely. Advancement with such an organ-isation tends to depend not on merit, but on long service.
>
> The organic type of organisation, on the other hand, is designed to adapt to a rapid rate of change, to situations in which new and unfamiliar problems continually arise which cannot be broken down and distributed among the existing specialist roles. Relationships are therefore lateral rather than vertical, and form and reform according to the demands of the particular problem. Innovation may occur at any level, and will be a product of the greater commit-ment to and understanding of the overall aims of the organisation.
>
> (Poster 1976: 4–5)

However advantageous might be an organisational structure capable of util-ising the management skills of more teachers within the school, thus giving them a sense of ownership of the process, existing mechanistic structures could not become organic by decree. Indeed, change had to begin at the top and demonstrate its effectiveness to the staff as a whole before it became acceptable. There was insufficient recognition at this early stage of the warning that any organisation is the simultaneous working of at least three social systems. The first of these is the formal authority system derived from the aims of the organisation. . . . But organisations are also cooperative systems of people who have career ambitions and a career structure. . . . [Finally] every organisation is the scene of 'political' activity in which individuals and departments compete and cooperate for power.

(Burns and Stalker 1968: 46–7)

Those few headteachers opening new comprehensive schools and able to hand-pick many of their teachers were better placed to set up structures that leaned towards the organic. Others, attempting to impose radical change on existing structures and practices, learnt the hard way that haste must be made slowly.

The curriculum explosion

The distinction, in Hughes' typology, between the traditionalist and the innovator was by the 1970s no longer wholly within the headteacher's control. In England and Wales the newly established Schools Council was promoting widespread curricular innovation. Interestingly, in view of the future centralisation of the primary and secondary curriculum, the Council's 'projects and reports were largely permissive [rather] than prescriptive, reflecting a view that curriculum innovation should be based on individual schools and led by teachers' (Holmes and McLean 1989: 44).

Why did schools engage so readily in curricular innovation? First, there was often start-up money available, for books, materials, equipment and additional staff. That the time would inevitably come when there was to be no further pump-priming was rarely considered. Second, there were external pressures. District boards and LEAs keen to be seen in the forefront of change invited schools, often those already successfully involved in innovation in other fields, to participate. Within the school the head of a successful faculty or department, influenced by career prospects in an expanding market, might well be a powerful advocate of change in his or her specialism. Principals and headteachers were often ill-placed to evaluate the merits of a proposal. Alternatively, they might exert pressure on curriculum leaders, believing that innovation would add to the school's prestige.

The result was that innovating schools, in England and Wales as in the USA, were inundated with paper and therefore forced into the organisational domain when their prime concerns ought to have been with the managerial domain.

In this same period, following the *Beloe Report* (1963), the Certificate of Secondary Education (CSE) was launched in England and Wales. It was based on regional examination boards and was predominantly teacher-led. The CSE met a need that had been growing year by year in secondary modern and comprehensive schools for an examination suitable for those for whom the General Certificate in Education (GCE), designed for the top 20 per cent of the ability range, was deemed inappropriate. Apart from obvious benefits to the pupils, what this innovation achieved was the cross-fertilisation of ideas and standards among schools, through standardisation meetings and the marking of coursework.

It is unlikely that the effect on the management structure of the comprehensive school of the empowerment of department heads and their subject teams could have been foreseen. Headteachers could no longer maintain control of the examination curriculum in the same way as they could when the school was dealing with the published syllabuses of examination boards. When a relatively small proportion of the comprehensive school population was destined to sit the GCE examination, then banding was an obvious form of pupil organisation. Now that the majority of pupils who remained after the then minimum leaving age of 15 were examination candidates, some in varying combinations of GCE and CSE, others in a wide range of CSE options, the managerial power base had shifted towards subject specialists. Nor was it only in the subject field that radical change was taking place. The tutor's role had to extend from a concern for caring and good behaviour to that of guidance on subject and examination choice. Unless headteachers saw their new role as providers of support for these developing trends in decentralised responsibility rather than themselves single-handedly 'running a tight ship', the school would not cope with change and staff would become disillusioned.

This period of curriculum development, which was to continue well into the next decade, marked a significant step forward in management practice, in that the demands of change in any one area of a school's activity affected the entire organisation and could no longer be treated in isolation. Needless to say, many headteachers also required in-service training in their new leadership role.

The growth of participative management

The growing interest among headteachers in management theory led some to consider their own leadership style. For this they needed to become better acquainted with management research, the outcomes of which were fortunately easy to apply to headship, even though they had been conceived in the managerial terms encountered in business and industrial management literature. Tannenbaum and Schmidt (1973) expanded their earlier four styles – tells, sells, consults, joins – and now identified seven different styles of management. The manager:

12

- makes a decision and then announces it;
- makes a decision and then sells it to staff;
- presents ideas to staff and invites questions;
- presents a tentative decision, subject to modification;
- presents a problem to staff and selects from their suggested solutions;
- identifies the problem, leaving staff to make the decision;
- leaves staff to identify the problem and make the decision.

Today, we need to be wary of classifying in a way which suggests a 'best style', and consider the appropriateness of each style to a particular circumstance. Hersey and Blanchard (1982) proposed the theory of situational leadership and posited that leadership behaviour, which now seemed the better term, depended on the maturity of subordinates. There are, they stated, two dimensions of maturity, each important to situational leadership: professional maturity and psychological maturity. While recognition of the link between task and relationship remains important, matching the leadership behaviour to the situation is of no less value for effective management.

No change in leadership style or behaviour could of itself meet all emerging needs of the 1970s and 1980s. Many comprehensive schools began to look at their structures and to seek ways of adapting them to the complex demands of management. In large schools, the weight of administration that had little or nothing to do with the learning and caring within the institution was inhibiting headteachers from effective action. Such schools needed ancillary staff trained in administrative skills. Local education authorities were slow to see the importance of making provision for appointments to such posts, but headteachers with experienced postholders in administration soon realised that, relieved of routine maintenance tasks, they were better able to apply themselves to developing effective management structures.

As the curriculum–pastoral divide was seen to be more and more unreal when almost all subject teachers were also pastoral tutors, a closer relationship between senior managers became imperative. The notion of the senior management team, consisting of the headteacher and deputies, and perhaps two or three others, usually representative of curricular and pastoral interests, became more common. The full staff meeting was increasingly recognised as a poor forum for the dissemination of information, better done verbally or in writing, and, in large schools, an even poorer forum for discussion. Smaller groups were better able to promote good management practices, and the creation of *ad hoc* committees to consider and make recommendations on a particular aspect of curriculum development or pastoral care was one way of achieving this. With the rapid expansion of comprehensive education, in-house training for posts of greater seniority, whether in one school or a group of schools, arose exponentially.

13

Leadership was beginning to move closer to the collaborative style so essential to the development towards restructuring, as will be seen in Chapter 3. The pyramidal structure was increasingly replaced by a central core from which radiated a number of pods, with defined powers of decision making. Nevertheless, however valuable this diversification of responsibility might be, without a clear overview from the centre a school would be in danger of the fragmentation of its purpose. The need for the establishment of monitoring and evaluation routines was becoming apparent.

The growth of parental involvement

Traditionally, schools communicated with parents by sending short written reports at the end of each term. For working-class parents to come to the school to discuss academic or behavioural shortcomings of their child was a rarity. The publication of the Newsom Report (1963) and the Plowden Report (1967) had marked the beginning of a change in attitude which was to bear fruit in the 1970s:

> Plowden acknowledges parents as partners, with a much more than peripheral part to play in the process of education. A whole section of the report is concerned with the home, school and neighbourhood and there is a complete chapter on participation by parents . . . stressing the influence of parental attitudes on educational performance.
>
> (Cave 1970: 63)

The first significant change was the growing practice of report evenings, when in timed interviews the tutor would discuss with parents, and increasingly with their children present, the contents of the report. Indicative of the importance of this type of parent evening was the increased attendance of working-class parents, and of both parents. There is little research evidence for this in the 1970s, but at workshops and conferences of schools promoting home–school relations there was much anecdotal evidence. In some schools, primary and secondary, pupils were being given the task of negotiating with teachers an interview schedule for their parents, enhancing pupil involvement and saving parents' time.

Towards a policy for in-service education

Busy teachers, with time for personal study at a premium, looked for suitable courses on management, and found many of them less than satisfactory. It was becoming obvious that there was a need to alter the traditional approach – that of taught courses with a strong bent towards academic learning – of a majority of in-service providers. During the 1970s neither the DES nor the

LEAs had a clear picture of the efficacy or even the methodology of in-service courses in education management for teachers. Accordingly, in 1979 the DES commissioned from the University of Birmingham a survey with the expressed aim of obtaining 'a clearer picture of provision' and thereby having 'a firmer basis for policy making by central and local government in relation to future provision' (Hughes *et al.* 1982: 2).

Within a year of the publication of this report the DES had taken two decisive initiatives to advance education management training nationally. The first was the promulgation of DES *Circular 3/83*, providing educational management courses of two types: one-term training opportunities (OTTO) for headteachers of considerable experience; and basic (twenty-day minimum) courses for senior staff. Next came the funding by the DES of the National Development Centre for School Management Training (NDC) as a joint activity of the School of Education of the University of Bristol and the South West Management Centre of Bristol Polytechnic (now the University of the West of England).

The one-term training opportunities often had no taught component except when there were, within the current advanced degree programme of the institution, lectures and discussions appropriate to the outcome of the secondment. Some outcomes were of a very high standard, particularly when the purpose of the secondment had been clearly thought through by the parties involved. The twenty-day courses were far more variable in standard, despite NDC course criteria and DES monitoring. Some of the best courses demonstrated a real understanding of the benefit of having an industrial consultant or trainer on the planning committee. Everard and Marsden (1985: 50), trainers with wide experience of the spheres of both education and industry, succinctly identified the major issue for schools:

> In the past, education management courses have mainly focused on 'administration', or the management of the status quo but, as society becomes more turbulent, managers are increasingly expected to steer their organisations towards new goals. The capacity for managing change is less well developed than it is in parts of industry which have faced the need for major reconstruction as a result of market changes.

There is no doubt that, in terms of numbers at least, the three-year period of intensive funding for management training for headteachers and senior staff made a decided impact: one in three secondary schools and one in ten primary schools benefited from the DES initiative. Whether the quality of the provision enabled all or most participating schools to become more effective is open to question. Hellawell (1984) writes of the identification of five 'ideal types' against which management training courses might be set. The one most applicable to OTTO and twenty-day courses was 'to develop general areas of competence', for the most part competence in administration. What was absent, and remained absent in many training institutions right into the present decade, were courses 'designed to enhance the principal's self-concept and to promote self-realisation' (ibid.: 52). School effectiveness is unlikely to be achieved solely through self-realisation, but it is a valuable starting-point towards the management of change.

The introduction of appraisal

The beginnings of the introduction of appraisal for all were not auspicious. The Education (No. 2) Act of 1986 set the scene for the introduction of appraisal in a formula of words symptomatic of the way in which decision making in national educational issues was being dictated by central government at this time – without adequate consultation or preparation:

> The Secretary of State may by regulations make provision for requiring LEAs or such other persons as may be prescribed to secure that the performance of teachers to whom the regulations apply . . . is regularly appraised in accordance with such regulations as may be prescribed.
>
> (DES 1986a)

Teachers and LEAs agreed that they wanted from appraisal

> a continuous and systematic process intended to help individual teachers with their professional development and career planning, and to help ensure that the in-service training and deployment of teachers match the complementary needs of individual teachers and the schools.
>
> (ACAS 1986)

There was a further concern, well-founded in the event, that there would not be adequate funding either for the training of appraisers and appraisees, both initially and as staff changes took place, or to meet the time costs of the implementation, year by year, of the appraisal process.

As the appraisal process had as a major remit the promotion of staff development, there was a growing recognition that this could best be achieved through the wider adoption by agreement of managerial responsibilities, whether task-oriented or expressive, that would enhance teacher concern for and involvement in the running of the school.

Perhaps the most significant outcome of the introduction of appraisal was that it promoted in many schools a more holistic approach to school management, of a kind that would more readily respond to the demands and opportunities of the school-effectiveness movement of the late 1980s and the 1990s' practice of restructuring.

The governance of schools

Baron and Howell (1974) found that section 20 of the 1944 Education Act, which allowed LEAs to group schools under one management body, 'had been used to an extent which went far beyond what one presumes to be the authors' intentions' (Sallis 1988: 111). In the county boroughs, as they then were, one-quarter had a single body as managers/governors for all their primary and secondary schools. Membership was by education committee appointment and often consisted mainly of councillors or political appointees. It was time for a change, and a report was commissioned. The Taylor Report (1977) *A New Partnership for Our Schools* had as its terms of reference:

> To review the arrangements for the management and government of maintained primary and secondary schools in England and Wales, including the composition and functions of bodies of managers and governors, and their relationship with headteachers and staff of schools, with parents of pupils, and with the local community at large, and to make recommendations.

The three basic principles described in the Preface to the report were:

> Equal partnership in the constitution of governing bodies; the responsibility of those bodies for the success of the school in all aspects of its life and work; and their duty to promote good relationships and effective communication both within the school and between the school and its parents and community.
>
> (Cited Sallis 1988: 181–2)

The first government response to the Taylor Report came not from the Labour government, which had commissioned it, but from the Conservative government which was elected in 1979. The response took the form of the Education Act 1980 and the subsequent Statutory Instrument 809/81 which, while not specifically taking up the recommendations of the Taylor Report, nevertheless dealt with a number of issues affecting the governance of schools. There was, for example, some amelioration of the restrictive conditions which governed the constitution and powers of governing bodies, but there was little substantive change.

It may be that the Conservative government wanted time to bring about its own version of the enlargement of the role of schools' governing bodies, as it did in the Education (No. 2) Act of 1986. Almost all of the Taylor

Committee's recommendations, nine years after it submitted its report, had become law. Within a further two years, before the newly elected governing bodies had settled in, the Education Reform Act (DES 1988) fundamentally changed the responsibilities of governors, especially through the introduction of local financial management (LFM) and local management of schools (LMS).

The growth of centralised control

Financial delegation to schools, or local financial management as it was to be called, did not originate in the provisions of the Education Reform Act of 1988. The phase III Leicestershire Community Colleges piloted block-budgeting from 1978 and were able to resource school and community activities within the same budget, subject to the authority of the governing body, on which the community councils were represented. Cambridgeshire had in 1982 initiated a trial scheme for LFM which became the prototype for the financial element of the self-managing school.

The Chartered Institute of Public Finance and Accountancy (1988) had outlined four criteria for the successful implementation of local management of schools: 'good management training [of school staff and governors]; sound planning; good communication; positive attitudes'. In respect of LFM the major stumbling block was that, so rapidly did the government require the implementation of this scheme, there was time for only the most perfunctory training; and on good management training the other three CIPFA criteria depended absolutely.

Those schools, primary and secondary, with non-teaching ancillary staff competent in budgetary control were much advantaged. Nevertheless, even when the monitoring of budgetary expenditure could be undertaken by a member of the non-teaching staff, the whole field of budgetary planning became at the first level the responsibility of the headteacher, and at the overview level that of the finance committee of the governing body. Few headteachers had the skills required for creating and maintaining an annual and a rolling budget; training was of necessity brief, often with compendious documentation, and few governing bodies had the financial expertise to monitor the headteacher's decisions. Allocating capitation had been relatively easy. Now staff costs, building repairs, the employment of supply teachers, all had to be budgeted for, however unpredictable these headings might be. Overspending was an ever-present nightmare, with governors ultimately responsible. Now the LEA was required by the 1988 Education Reform Act to delegate the greater part of the education committee's budget, reserving only a small, and declining, percentage for the provision of centralised resources; there was no possibility of an appeal for extra funds.

Local management of schools (LMS) – that is, the empowerment of the governing body – appeared to have much to recommend it. Regrettably, the government's keenness to introduce it was motivated by ideological rather than by managerial considerations, as the thin edge of the wedge towards the creation of a competitive market economy for schools. This stems from a politico-economic belief in the efficiency of free economic markets to deliver goods and services effectively and provide consumers with choice. In a few short years market forces were to become the cornerstone of government ideology. There were to be yet more government-imposed changes: the introduction of the National Curriculum and the frequent modifications of its syllabus content; externally devised Key Stage tests at ages 7, 11 and 14; the results of these and of external examinations to be made public through league tables; the imposition on schools of a four-yearly external inspection by the Office for Standards in Education (OFSTED). If state schools were to survive in this demoralising climate, they needed to convey to parents that 'competition for excellence' was not the answer. Becoming a more effective school clearly was. The movement towards school improvement and school effectiveness is described in Chapter 2.

2

SCHOOL IMPROVEMENT AND SCHOOL EFFECTIVENESS

Introduction

In a symposium entitled *Making Good Schools*, Hopkins and Lagerweij (1996: 62–4) refer to the centralisation–decentralisation quandary as

> seemingly contradictory pressures for centralisation (increasing government control over policy and direction) on the one hand, and decentralisation (more responsibility for implementation, resource management and evaluation at the local level) on the other.

This tension, they argue, makes it difficult for schools to 'implement successfully innovations that make a real difference to the quality of schooling and pupil achievement'. There needs to be found an equilibrium between these two polarities, 'the centrally determined policy initiatives and the encouragement of locally developed school improvement efforts'.

The OECD (1989) report *Decentralisation and School Improvement* pointed out that

- new roles and responsibilities arise for schools and local authorities from decentralisation, that as a consequence tensions inevitably develop, and that means must be found to respond to these tensions;
- central authority has a responsibility to ensure that those undertaking new responsibilities are trained and supported; and
- any strategy for the management of change requires its consideration as a dynamic and evolutionary process, following from a clear vision of the expected results.

A significant factor in the centralise–decentralise debate is the relationship between research projects and practice.

Defining school improvement

Rutter *et al.* (1979) made it clear, throughout their detailed research findings of what actually took place in the classroom and the school, that certain qualitative factors result in enhanced student outcomes. Principal among these are those factors internal to the school:

- emphasis on the teaching–learning process, where there is a communality of approach within the staff of the school;
- management-led agreement on goals;
- a supportive learning climate, which includes soundly based relationships with parents; and
- high expectations of academic achievement and the growth of social competence.

Yet, widely read and commended as this research was, the feeling persists that good schools would find in it reinforcement for their good practices, and ineffective schools would not know how to introduce and implement the necessary qualitative changes.

The central definition of school improvement that was to be elaborated for the project was that of 'a systematic, sustained effort aimed at change in learning conditions and other related internal conditions in one or more schools, with the aim of accomplishing educational goals more effectively' (van Velzen *et al.* 1985: 48). The phrase 'one or more schools' might seem somewhat inappropriate to an international project, since small-scale change is hardly likely to have a serious impact on the quality of a national school system. Yet those who worked within and on the fringes of the project were well aware of the need to hold together a wide range of differing systems, some of which were more local or regional than national, and others of which lacked the resources and infrastructure to influence their schools as a whole.

School improvement as a vehicle of educational change rests on a number of assumptions, articulated by van Velzen *et al.* (1985) and Hopkins (1987, 1990), and summarised in Hopkins and Lagerweij (1996):

- The school is the centre of change.
- There is a systematic approach to change.
- The 'internal conditions' of schools are a key focus for change.
- Educational goals are accomplished more effectively.
- There is a multi-level perspective.
- Implementation strategies are integrated.
- There is a drive towards institutionalism.

The International School Improvement Project had worked through six representative area groups: school-based review for self-improvement; school leaders and the organisational development of schools; the role of external support; research and evaluation; development and implementation of school improvement policies by education authorities; and conceptual mapping of school improvement. The working methods of the ISIP were radically different from those of most educational conferences or projects: case studies; field visits; one-topic, in-depth seminars; collaborative, transnational pilot schemes; mutual consultation and assistance within and outside of formal project meetings; and, as outcomes, one or more publications from each of the area groups, overseen by a publications committee to ensure coherence.

The UK government's response, expressed by Halsey, the then Deputy Secretary of the DES, in his chapter 'Implications for school improvement in the United Kingdom' (in Hopkins 1987) was muted. There was no indication of how school improvement might be promoted, other than through vapid generalisations and exhortation, with one exception:

> Even the GCSE . . . will not be able to assess and record all the positive achievements of school pupils. The government has therefore set a further objective: the national introduction by the end of the decade of arrangements for providing all school leavers with records of achievement. It is intended that these will cover a much wider range of experience and achievements than can be tested in public examinations.
>
> (Halsey 1987: 177)

In the event, the Conservative government's concern for quantitative measures of success, expressed in Key Stage attainment levels and league tables of school performance in tests, public examinations and attendance, superseded the function of records of achievement.

Defining school effectiveness

The school-effectiveness movement predates the ISIP by a decade or more. Because there was no central funding to promote a coherent study of effectiveness, the early research findings were fragmentary and uncoordinated. Creemers (1996: 40) sums up what he entitles 'the first generation of school effectiveness studies' by extrapolating the factors most often mentioned in these studies:

- strong educational leadership
- high expectations of student achievement
- an emphasis on basic skills
- a safe and orderly climate
- frequent evaluation of pupil progress.

22

The second generation of school-effectiveness research and development saw a number of major studies, principally in England, the USA and the Netherlands. Mortimore *et al.* (1988) conducted a four-year research project on the academic and social progress of 2,000 primary children in fifty randomly selected London schools. Those schools which were effective in both spheres led the researchers to define the following characteristics of an effective school:

- the purposeful leadership of the staff by the headteacher;
- the involvement of the deputy in policy decision making and of the teaching staff in curriculum planning and certain areas of decision making;
- staff consistency in the approach to teaching, intellectually challenging teaching, structured sessions that nevertheless allowed students some freedom within the structure, and a limited focus within sessions;
- a work-centred environment, where there was the maximum communication between teachers and students;
- sound record-keeping procedures, effective monitoring of progress;
- parental involvement in schools which encouraged an open door policy;
- a positive climate.

In the USA there now were a number of major studies which sought to identify the significant differences between effective and ineffective schools. The most extensive of these studies was the Louisiana School Effectiveness Study, the findings of which largely replicated and reinforced the study (1988) by Mortimore *et al.*

Those involved in the school-effectiveness movement saw the need for the creation of a comprehensive model of educational effectiveness. Scheerens (1992) had emphasised the school level and Creemers (1994) the classroom level. They accepted that there is 'a formal relationship between what goes on in classrooms and between class and the school level' and that underpinning this relationship are 'the concepts of consistency, cohesion, constancy and control' (Creemers 1996: 49). The emphasis of school effectiveness was, and is, directed particularly towards what will be seen in Chapter 3 as the 'central variables'.

Reconciling the two fields of study

Whatever was, or more precisely was not, happening at governmental levels in England and Wales to promote school improvement, it is clear that most of the leading European and American educationalists involved in ISIP had no intention of letting the benefits of a four-year collaborative project disintegrate. These leaders recognised that:

- [S]chool improvement is very arid if it does not take into account that [it] is a multi-level process. . . . It is simply not enough to look at just one level of the system or to talk only with persons in a specific position in the school system, say, school leaders or politicians. All images . . . based on just one level, with just one perspective, will be flat, dead and useless.
- [W]e have to be aware of the fact that the school is the unit of change. . . . Whatever [school development is being planned] at the policy level . . . or by a single teacher in his or her classroom, sooner or later any improvement activity has to be bound up with the school as a unit.
- [S]chool improvement ultimately is not produced by models, planning schemes, regulations or even ISIP books, but by people working in that unit of change, the school.

(Bollen 1989: 11–12)

It is interesting to observe that these three statements, and particularly the first, foreshadow the holistic approach of restructuring.

Immediately following the conclusion of the formal OECD project, the Foundation for International Collaboration on School Improvement (FICSI) was founded, with the secretariat headquarters in the Netherlands. The task set when ISIP was inaugurated was by no means complete. At one level there was the need to continue with the publication of the task group findings. Furthermore, there was

> the recognition of the development of a strong network of individuals and institutions often linked to national authorities. . . . Within this network there was continued contact [and] exchange with ISIP colleagues. But a network is a very loosely coupled organisation and is bound to disintegrate over time unless it [is] stimulated at regular intervals by shared activities.

(Bollen 1989: 13)

Consequently, there took place in 1989 the first FICSI conference with the prime aim of seeing whether an understanding of school improvement had been deepened since the conclusion of the International School Improvement Project. The fact that the conference attracted participants from twelve countries was an indication of a real need for an organisation to provide continuity and to update concepts in the light of experience and practice. The FICSI group met annually at the American Education Research Association (AERA) and shared research papers relevant to school improvement. However, there was already in existence the International Congress for School Effectiveness and Improvement (ICSEI), and the Foundation for International Collaboration on School Improvement decided to bridge the gap between the two academic schools of thought by presenting symposia at the ICSEI annual conferences.

> It was clear from these sessions that the 'effectiveness' people viewed school improvement operating on a modest empirical base that was weak and eclectic. By contrast, school 'improvement' people expressed surprise about the reluctance of effectiveness researchers to explore interventions within schools.
>
> (van den Hoven 1996: vi)

Despite this apparent polarisation of stances, dialogue between representatives of the two fields of research developed. Although the organisations remained distinct, a series of meetings beginning in 1993 explored the areas of difference and of common ground, one significant outcome of which was the publication in 1996 of Reynolds *et al.*'s *Making Good Schools: Linking School Effectiveness and School Improvement.*

Barth (1990) had categorised two different approaches to school reform that derive from different assumptions. The first, which he held to be the dominant approach, he describes thus:

- Schools do not have the capacity or the will to improve themselves; improvements must therefore come from sources outside the school.
- What needs to be improved about schools is the level of pupil performance and achievement, best measured by standardised tests.
- Schools can be found in which pupils are achieving beyond what might be predicted. By observing these schools, we can identify their characteristics as 'desirable'.
- Teachers and headteachers in other schools can be trained to display the desirable traits of their counterparts in high-achieving schools. Then their pupils too will excel.
- School improvement, then, is an attempt to identify what school people should know and be able to do and to devise ways to get them to do it.

(Barth 1990: 38)

In contrast, his alternative set of assumptions is described as follows:

- Schools have the capacity to improve themselves, if the conditions are right, [and] a major responsibility of those outside the school is to help provide these conditions for those on the inside.

- When the need and purpose are there, when the conditions are right, adults and students alike learn and each energises and contributes to the learning of the other.
- What needs to be improved about schools is their culture, the quality of interpersonal relationships, and the nature and quality of learning experiences.
- School improvement is an effort to determine and provide, from within and without, conditions under which the adults and youngsters who inhabit schools will promote and sustain learning among themselves.

(Barth 1990: 45)

Hopkins *et al*. (1994: 4) describe this first set of assumptions as that of the 'list makers'. These writers believe that the second set, basing school reform 'on the skills, aspirations and energy of those closest to the school: teachers, senior management, governors and parents' is more effective and 'captures the essence of [the] approach to school improvement'. It will be seen in the next chapter that the second set has some affinities with restructuring, though the criteria of the latter for achieving school improvement and effectiveness are far more comprehensive.

The notion of effective leadership

As a criterion for both school improvement and school effectiveness, the notion of leadership is of paramount importance. The term 'the school leader' appears frequently in the literature throughout the 1990s. Hopkins and Lagerweij (1996: 73) define the leader's attributes as follows:

The school leader has to show capacities [such] as functioning as a leader and innovator, being able to tell how changes can be applied in practice, being able to determine the scope of change, the capacity of support and stimulation, and being able to develop skills to foster a learning organisation.

While one would not question the value of this set of attributes, it is important to recognise that, for the effective school and particularly at a time of rapid and extensive change, leadership needs to be a multi-level attribute, one that is as applicable to senior and middle management as to the headteacher.

As long ago as 1983 Adair formulated the idea of 'action-centred leadership'. His main premiss is that, for effective staff management, the team leader must attach equal importance to three essential factors: the task, the team, and the individuals in the team. It is clear that one is thus no longer tied to the top-down model which dominated the management of many of the schools in the periods described in Chapter 1. Leadership may come from any level of management depending on the nature of the task. Moreover, both the team and the individual are involved in decision making, and thus are not passive recipients of directives from the leadership. Corporate leadership is a term that has been much misunderstood, sometimes much abused. It is not an abdication of the leader's responsibility, but an extension of that responsibility to the membership of the team. The checklist (Table 2.1), adapted by Dunham (1995) from Adair (1983), makes clear the responsibility of the leader to the team and to each individual member at each stage of the management process.

It is vital, but not always well understood, that leadership is not simplistically equated with management. Gardner (1990: 1) makes clear that leadership is 'the process of persuasion or example by which an individual (or leadership team) induces a group to pursue objectives held by the leader or shared by the leader and his or her followers'.

Managers are those individuals who hold 'a directive post in an organisation presiding over the resources by which the organisation functions, allocating resources prudently, and making the best possible use of people' (Dunham 1995: 3).

Burns (1978), writing primarily about industrial and commercial undertakings, distinguished between transactional and transformational

Table 2.1   Checklist on leadership role

Key stages	Task	Team	Individual
Define objectives	Identify tasks and constraints	Involve the team, share commitment	Clarify objectives, gain acceptance
Plan	Establish priorities, check resources, decide and set standards	Consult, encourage ideas and actions, develop suggestions and structure	Assess skills, set targets, delegate, persuade
Brief	Brief the team, check understanding	Answer questions, obtain feedback	Listen, enthuse
Support, monitor	Report progress, maintain standards and discipline	Coordinate, reconcile conflict	Advise, assist and reassure, recognise effort, counsel
Evaluate	Summarise progress, review objectives, replan if necessary	Recognise success, learn from failure	Assess performance, appraise, guide and train

Source: Adapted by Dunham (1995) from Adair (1983).

leadership. Broadly speaking, the former concentrates on managing what is, the latter on change, innovation and entrepreneurship. Hord (1992: 22–3) summarises the transactional leader as one who

> changes and transforms the organisation according to a vision of a preferred status. Leaders . . . are change makers and transformers, guiding the organisation to a new and more compelling vision, a demanding role expectation.

However, it is easy, in considering what makes an effective school, to be deceived by the visionary concept of transformational leadership into diminishing the need for transactional leadership. The emphasis of the latter, as Stoll and Fink (1996: 105) point out, is

> primarily about the management of school structure. It involves focusing on purposes of the organisation, developing plans, ensuring task completion, facilitating information flow, and working well with the various school groups. . . . These factors are necessary to maintain effectiveness.

Leithwood (1992: 9) rightly observes that transactional and transformational leadership are 'often viewed as complementary', with transactional practices needed to ensure that the day-to-day routines are carried out, but he maintains that transactional practices do not stimulate improvement. This is certainly true; but unless transactional practices are in place, clearly understood and supported by all concerned, transformation will be difficult to achieve and may even be nullified.

Stoll and Fink (1996: 109–17) argue convincingly and at length for 'invitational leadership'. They quote the contention of Purkey and Novak (1990): 'People behave in ways consistent with their concept of self. . . . Invitations, therefore, are messages communicated to people which inform them that they are able, responsible and worthwhile.' Invitational leaders demonstrate optimism, respect and trust, and their actions are intentionally supportive, caring and encouraging.

The importance of the personal qualities of school leaders is reinforced by the view that, to transform their schools, school leaders must use facilitative rather than authoritarian power. Leithwood (1992: 9–10) claims that they do this by

- helping staff members develop and maintain a collaborative professional school structure;
- fostering teacher development;
- helping staff solve problems together more effectively.

In the UK Handy (1985) was an early and powerful advocate of moving consideration of leadership away from situational approaches towards behavioural theories. Writing about all organisations, but described here for schools by Dennison and Shenton (1987: 38), Handy posits four groups of influencing factors which any leader needs to consider

- the professional style and personal characteristics of the school leadership;
- the style of leadership preferred by the staff, and the dependence of this on circumstances;
- the task: that is, the job, its objectives and the associated technology;
- the environment: that is, the organisational situation of the headteacher and the staff group in relation to the importance of the task.

Fidler offers for consideration Bolman and Deal's (1991) fourfold typology of leadership—structural, human relations, political and symbolic:

> Each style has advantages but should not be regarded as exclusive. ... The result of analysing the leader's [preferred or dominant] style and comparing this with the needs of the organisation at that particular time may throw up additional requirements in order for the organisation to be successful.
>
> (Fidler 1996: 75)

Competence-based approaches

The first significant indication that competence-based approaches might be appropriate to school management development came from the work of the School Management Task Force (1990). Earley (1992, 1993) built on this initiative to identify precisely the definition and content of competences appropriate to effective management.

Earley points out that there have been two definitions of competences:

> the characteristics of effective or 'superior' managers, and the actual performance required of managers. The former definition, derived from North America, gives much importance to the personal competences that individuals bring with them to the job and sees competence as 'the predisposition to behave in ways associated with the achievement of successful performance'. The latter definition stresses outcomes and 'the ability to perform work to the standards required in employment'.
>
> (Easley 1993: 144)

While personal qualities are not unimportant in school leadership, effective management requires that

> management standards centre on the requirements of the managerial role to be performed rather than on individual managers and the attributes they should possess. Standards attempt to provide specifications or benchmarks against which the performance of managers or management teams can be assessed. Performance criteria define explicitly what is expected of effective performance at work.
>
> (ibid.)

The Management Charter Initiative (MCI) identified four key managerial roles: operations, finance, people and information. It broke these down into a total of ten units of management competence, each of which is subdivided into elements consisting of performance criteria against which individuals and teams must provide evidence for assessment (Day 1990). However, the MCI standards were created for the purpose of accreditation and certification, and as such were considered too generic to be entirely appropriate to schools. Consequently, there have been several projects, notably by School Management South and the University of Wolverhampton, to refine the work of the MCI. The four key roles in these two projects were redefined as the management of policy, of learning, of people, of resources.

Earley identified a number of ways in which competence statements might be used in schools, of which the most important for the promotion of school effectiveness and school improvement are

- as a self-reflective and self-assessment tool
- as the basis for job descriptions
- as part of the appraisal process
- for school review and institutional development.

(Earley 1993: 147)

A major problem in the use of competences is that their very complexity may deter busy schools from making use of them. The University of Wolverhampton School Management Competences Project, for example, proceeds from the mission statement to the four key functions, then the ten units of competence (subdivisions of the key functions).

> Beyond this there are further divisions, called elements, performance criteria and range indicators. These, while appropriate to a finely tuned exploration and evaluation of the management of an educational institution, are beyond the basic needs of the appraisal process.
>
> (Poster and Poster 1993: 179)

Earley (1993: 149) strikes a sensible balance by indicating that a competence-based approach is only one of a number of developmental strategies.

Team culture and effective schools

What Handy (1988) described as the shift from the power culture to the team culture is an essential feature of the development of effective schools. In the former, the ability of the school leader is essential to an understanding of how the organisation functions, because all direction and control radiates outwards. This appeared to work in the past, when centralised decision making was expected and accepted by the staff of the school, because all or most lacked relevant leadership experience. It is no longer appropriate to the complexity of demands made upon a school, whatever its size, or to the aspirations and expectations of many of the new generation of teachers.

In the team culture, specialist groups or teams come together to solve cross-curricular problems or achieve specific multi-disciplinary objectives. When they have completed their task they may be disbanded or their composition reviewed for a further, cognate task. There is a growing practice for responsibility for a one-off task to be agreed with a member of staff, even though this may not appear within the role definition, and even for that person to consult with or gather together a team of teachers of his or her own choice. In this culture staff are likely to be enthusiastic contributors whatever the defined levels of responsibility, and there is likely to be development, of both the individual and the organisation.

The idea of the role of the school leader has changed radically from that which was common, indeed nearly universal, in the prevalent management style considered in Chapter 1. The team culture, usually made manifest in terms of collaborative or corporate management, is far from being a universal feature in our schools, but there is movement, admittedly unquantifiable, in this direction if only because of the need for the management load to be spread. This is a pragmatic argument for corporate management, largely for transactional reasons. However, Fullan (1992: 20) develops the transformational aspect, arguing that good school leaders do not create a vision independently and impose it on people, but rather develop a collaborative structure in which participants build a vision together. The evolution of a visionary approach through transformational leadership becomes even more pertinent as the school-effectiveness movement develops into the restructuring process, as Chapter 3 reveals.

Quality in education

'Quality' is a term that, until recently, has been used in education with little real precision and mainly as a 'hurrah' word.

31

There can be no absolute definition of quality. Quality management is concerned with fitness of purpose: while the central purpose of a school, as encapsulated in its mission statement, will hold good, there will be external and internal forces that determine changes in the aims and objectives and modify the steps that need to be taken to achieve quality.

It is as well to be clear about the terminology whereby different aspects of quality management are defined: quality control, quality assurance and total quality management.

Quality control (QC) takes place *after* the process, which in education happens most frequently through external inspection. Its value is that it enables the school to take steps to remedy shortcomings; its principal weakness is that it implies a top-down model of management which tends to diminish the responsibility of those in the school immediately involved, the very people who are most likely to know the causes of those shortcomings and the rate at and means by which they can be remedied.

Quality assurance (QA) takes place *before* and *during* the process. It aims to prevent failure by setting in advance clear standards of performance in the planning of which all those responsible for the process are involved. Its principal shortcoming is that management may become self-satisfied and carry the same standards forward year by year without reconsidering them, simply because they have been successful in the past. Yet, as West-Burnham (1993: 167) points out, this is unlikely to happen if

> quality consists in meeting the requirements, specifications or needs of a customer or client. For many organisations this represents a culture shift away from 'we know what quality is' to 'your requirements are our only definition of quality'.

Whether schools fall within the category of organisations whose mission is to meet the requirements of the client is debatable. The needs of primary clients, the students, are determined in part by societal requirements, in that one goal of school education is to equip them for employment, higher and further education and lifelong learning. Other important needs are determined by government, particularly through the medium of the National Curriculum.

Total quality management (TQM) takes place *before*, *during* and *after* the process, and throughout the school. Clear standards of performance are set through unambiguous written statements of expectation, and both the standards themselves and the processes are regularly reviewed and improved by all concerned.

> People are trusted to work as professionals, and there is a strong emphasis on teamwork. In contrast there is a weak emphasis on hierarchy. Critically, the organisation sets clear goals which are

communicated effectively. As a consequence, every member of the organisation has high expectations of themselves.

(Blandford 1997: 21)

Since quality is the responsibility of everybody in the school, staff development is an essential feature of TQM, and ongoing monitoring and evaluation are important to the health of the organisation. Since TQM is a holistic approach to management, its relevance to restructuring can be readily appreciated.

Most schools have quality assurance systems for some aspects of the school's life – the issues are comprehensiveness across the school and consistency over time. In order to achieve these elements a number of practical steps can be taken, according to West-Burnham (1993: 171–2), such as:

- a clear commitment to quality in the mission statement and a policy for managing quality;
- a quality manual which outlines the specific components of how the school will manage quality;
- a clear definition of the responsibility of every individual to deliver quality to every client on every occasion;
- the development of 'contracts' to confirm the mutual obligations of supplier and customer;
- the establishment of 'standard operating procedures' – schemes of work, marking schemes, etc. – to help deliver consistency;
- the use of quality audits to establish the integrity of provision against specification.

There are two elements of TQM which, while originating in industry, are of increasing interest and application to the management of the effective school. The first is the national standard Investors in People, based on the experience of many successful UK companies. Such companies have all found that their performance has been improved by a planned approach to:

- setting and communicating organisational goals
- developing their people to meet these goals, so that
- what people can do (and are motivated to do) matches what the organisation needs them to do.

(Barker 1993: 155)

The second is the British Standard (BS 5750), which is a detailed systems-based element of total quality management, the adaptation of which to schools has been undertaken jointly by the British Standards Institution and one of the case study schools (see Chapter 6). Both Investors in People and BS 5750 are gaining in popularity with the evolution of school management systems for effective schooling. That the latter has an annual review of the entitlement to continue to be credited with the kitemark, and the former a triennial review, may, along with the consideration of the far greater amount of time needed to document the case for the latter, influence schools towards IIP accreditation.

The effective school as a learning organisation

Professional development is an important feature of school improvement and effectiveness, and will play a central role in schools' and LEAs' endeavours to understand the processes of restructuring. Rudduck (1981) argued that

> the ultimate purpose of professional development is less to implement a specific innovation or policy and more to create individual and organisational habits and structures that make continuous learning a valued and endemic part of the culture of schools and teaching.

Craft (1996: 41) quotes Holly and Southworth (1989), who summarise the characteristics of the learning school as

- interactive and negotiative
- creative and problem solving
- proactive and responsive
- participative and collaborative
- flexible and challenging
- risk-taking and enterprising
- evaluative and reflective
- supportive and developmental.

If, Craft argues, these are the attributes of the learning policy for the school's students, then they should equally be the characteristics of effective professional development.

Conclusion

The development to restructuring from the school-improvement and effective-school movements is dealt with in Chapter 3. My contention is that piecemeal moves to effectiveness are unstable and highly vulnerable to external factors. What is required for sustained school effectiveness is not merely good leadership but a holistic approach which maintains the vital link between sound teaching and learning, on the one hand, and the management processes which will deliver them, on the other.

3

TRANSFORMING
SCHOOLS THROUGH
RESTRUCTURING

Introduction

As was shown in the previous chapter there has been during the 1990s a significant *rapprochement* between the aims of school improvement and school effectiveness, and the criteria for determining the extent to which a school is effective are, however differently expressed by change agents and researchers, well known. The focus is essentially on student achievement: 'in schools as places where primarily learning takes place, the objectives of education are primarily students' learning outcomes' (Creemers 1996: 32). Creemers concedes that these outcomes can be found not only in the cognitive domain but in the affective, social and aesthetic domains, but that, none the less, the cognitive objectives 'are crucial for the educational system in general' (ibid.: 33). Those who have in the same decade been exploring restructuring, both theoretically and in the field, would agree entirely with Creemers' view, not disputing the central importance of achievement in the cognitive domain but claiming that there are other factors which enhance learning and which must be taken into consideration if these objectives are to be attained. It is the sum total of these factors, as will become apparent in this chapter, which makes holism the crux of the theory and practice of restructuring.

It is therefore important to define from the beginning what restructuring is and what it is not:

> Restructuring involves changes in roles, rules, and relationships between and among students and teachers, teachers and administrators, and administrators at various levels from the school building to the district office to the state level, all with the aims of improving student outcomes.
>
> (Sashkin and Egermeier 1992: 3)

The use of the phrase 'rules, roles and relationships' derives, as will be seen later in this chapter, from the writings and practice of Corbett (1990).

35

Hopkins and Lagerweij (1996: 65), who cite Sashkin and Egermeier, point out that these authors

> outline four components of successful restructuring . . . the necessity to decentralise authority; a basic change in accountability; more student-focused and less teacher-centred instruction; and the development of new forms of testing that fit the curriculum and methods of instruction.

The connection between school improvement—effectiveness, on the one hand, and restructuring, on the other, is thus taking shape, though there remain significant differences. The two latter components align with what Conley (see p. 38) describes as 'the central variables', one element only of the three sets of variables that form his definition of restructuring. The first two components, on the other hand, reflect the changes in school management necessary for effective teaching and learning that were becoming apparent in Chapter 1.

Forces for change

The education of children should not be for society as we know it, but should aim to give them competence for the foreseeable future. The world in which schools currently exist is changing, and at an accelerating rate. The economic systems of all Western countries have been transformed. In the United Kingdom the near certainty of employment on leaving school has been replaced by a strong likelihood of unemployment, temporary or part-time employment, or employment below the learned skills and intellectual capacities of school and higher-education students.

Elmore *et al.* (1990: 2) indicate that those who may once have entered teaching now have access to other professions. In the USA the Holmes Group report on *Tomorrow's Teachers* concluded (1986: 31) that 'the traditions of recruitment, norms of preparation, and conditions of work in schools have severely hindered efforts to improve the quality of teaching', a view that, a decade later, would be endorsed in the UK by anyone seriously concerned about the state of our schools.

There is as yet little recognition in practice that the whole nature of academic attainment is evolving from the subject-based to the holistic. Learning needs to be integrated, not fragmented, and concerned more with 'how' and 'why' than with 'what'. Sir Geoffrey Holland, permanent secretary until 1994 at the then Department of Education, in a lecture to members of the Foundation for Manufacturing and Industry said:

> If we are honest with ourselves, the failure rate in our education system is one which would have long ago bankrupted any

commercial business or enterprise. The priority in schools should become learning rather than teaching. This will require a fundamental reversal of the role of the teacher, to be a supporter of the learner, an encourager, a facilitator, a mentor or guide.

(Guardian 20 November 1995)

There were at the beginning of the 1990s some excellent studies in the United States on what education should be about, and there was 'a marked degree of congruence between what the business community says it wants from workers and the qualities many educators might say they want to cultivate in students' (Conley 1993: 41). Conley then goes on to summarise what seem to be the main areas of agreement, the need for:

- curriculum that moves from a primary emphasis on rote learning and factual information to a greater emphasis on problem solving, application and integration of knowledge and higher-order thinking
- students who are actively engaged in learning, who are not being trained simply to do what they are told
- learning that is best assessed in terms of outcomes, not processes . . . the ability to apply or demonstrate a skill or set of knowledge as the best way to assess whether learning has really occurred
- education that extends beyond the walls of the classroom: students who apply knowledge and acquire new skills, information and insights in the larger community
- teachers who facilitate learning, not control it; one of the key goals of education being to create lifelong learners . . . not merely to transmit a body of information in a way that leaves the student with negative attitudes about learning
- students who learn to work in groups and as members of teams . . . and with students who are very different from themselves
- the belief that all learners are valuable [and have] positive self-images and the ability to define goals for themselves
- process skills considered as important as knowledge of specific content.

(Conley 1993: 41–2)

The irony of this is that much of what business leaders, here as in the USA, now consider to be desirable was derided by the late Conservative government for nearly two decades as 'progressive education', and dismissed as inappropriate to the needs of contemporary society.

Making the effective-school movement more effective

Initially, the central feature of the effective-school movement was the identification of the organisational factors that characterise effective schools. Schein (1985: 6) gives some common meanings of the word, which Hopkins *et al.* (1994) have extended with relevant examples:

- observed behavioural regularities when teachers interact in a staffroom – the language they use and the rituals they establish
- the norms that evolve in working groups of teachers in terms of lesson planning or monitoring the progress of students
- the dominant values espoused by a school
- the philosophy that, for example, guides the dominant approach to teaching and learning
- the rules of the game that new teachers have to learn in order to get along in the school or their department
- the feeling or climate that is conveyed by the entrance hall to a school, or the way in which students' work is or is not displayed.

(Hopkins *et al.* 1994: 88)

None of these, even with the examples added by Hopkins *et al.*, appear to be of themselves wholly satisfactory. What is needed is a holistic approach to school improvement that encompasses organisation factors, process factors and the culture of the effective school. Restructuring provides a means of profiling the totality of what constitutes the management of change.

Defining restructuring

The introduction to one of the earliest authoritative statements on restructuring (Corbett: 1990) made it clear that the term was already being used in the education management literature in the USA, though without any agreed definition. Corbett made a case for a workable definition by referring to the writings of the sociologist Wilson (1971), who argued that 'a social system's structure is a pattern of rules, roles and relationships'. This definition offers a new approach to analysing the processes of school management, particularly when the terms are further defined. Rules, in particular, may be misunderstood, without some elucidation. '[They] represent common understandings about what is and what ought to be' (Wilson 1971: 86–7). Rules may be realised in school policy documents and staff handbooks, and governmental curriculum directives, but unless they also 'embody the values and beliefs that professional educators (and parents) hold about schooling' (Corbett 1990: 3) they will be largely ineffective.

The use of the phrase 'what ought to be' is important. Vision is realised in the school's mission statement, and permeates the aims whereby that mission statement will be given effect. Without the maintenance of this vision a school may improve, but lack direction. 'Restructuring is systemic, and systemic change requires vision' (ibid.: 3). These three elements, *rules, roles* and *relationships*, are symbiotic. The introduction into the vocabulary of school management of job descriptions did much to remove the fuzziness that surrounded many school operations. In any organisation 'who does what' is not only a valuable safeguard; it supplies staff, parents, governors and the community with points of reference for information, clarification and decision making. Corbett makes the pertinent point that the expectations, both formal and informal, implicit in job descriptions concern both the responsibilities of the post-holder and the accepted ways in which those responsibilities will be carried out.

Precision in our understanding of the term 'relationships', as used by Wilson and advocated by Corbett, is essential. 'A social relationship can be said to exist only when, as a result of their common culture, one person's behavior elicits a dependable and expected response from another' (Wilson 1971: 88). This common culture does not come about by chance; it must be cultivated and is integral to the restructuring process. Fullan and Hargreaves (1992: 67) use the term 'collaborative cultures' to distinguish those which facilitate teacher development through mutual support, joint work and a broad agreement on educational values. In such schools 'the individual and the group are inherently and simultaneously valued'.

To Wilson's three sociological categories, Corbett (1990: 9–10) wisely, in the light of current concerns in the USA and England and Wales, adds a fourth: *results*. He makes it clear that, even though restructuring may lead to improved student performance in test scores, there must also be evidence of the way students learn. 'Student outcome measures, by themselves, are simply not useful for driving restructuring'; nor, one may add, for judging the effectiveness of schools. Corbett continues:

> While a restructuring [school] will clearly have differences in student outcomes in mind when it undertakes its effort, it will also focus on a variety of intermediate steps related to student and staff performance, the attainment of which [is] assumed to lead to improved student learning.
>
> (ibid.)

Restructuring must be defined. It has already been observed that one way in which to begin any definition is to define what it is not. This Raywid (1990a: 140–3) does succinctly. She differentiates three types of effort to improve schools: pseudo-reform, incremental reform and restructuring. She cites examples of pseudo-reform, all of which 'divert attention from more substantial reforms, and risk raising false hopes'. One widespread example is what she entitles 'symbolic politics'. She illustrates this from a survey of

high-school principals asked by Purkey *et al.* (1987) whether school improvement projects were going on in their schools:

> Then they surveyed teachers in those same schools about the char-
> acter of the projects reported. It seems that in more than half of the
> schools whose principals reported that improvement projects were
> under way, more than half the teachers were unaware of their exis-
> tence. . . . The creation of task forces is another pseudo-reform. 'It
> sometimes seems that convening the task force *is* the reform. . . .'
>
> (Raywid 1990a: 140–1)

Incremental reform is 'more ambitious in that it aims to improve educational practice'. The problem is that the improvement is invariably directed
at a particular group of students or a specific subject area. Apart from any
difficulties entailed in gaining approval for such a reform, funding it, planning it in detail, training staff to implement it, there remains one overriding
issue:

> Schools are notoriously difficult to change. One major reason that
> this is so is their interconnectedness. . . . In order to change
> almost anything of significance in schools, a great deal must be
> changed. . . . Schools are very much like jigsaw puzzles; everything
> is connected to everything else.
>
> (ibid.: 141)

Raywid states (1990a.: 142) that 'beginning in 1986 the excellence movement took a noticeable turn away from reform and toward restructuring'.
The date is that of two very important US reports (Carnegie Task Force
1986; National Governors' Association 1986), not to any significant state
or district implementation. The reports advocate major restructuring in
education which can be summarised as:

- changes in the way teaching and learning occur, or the core
  technology of schooling
- changes in the occupational situation of educators, including
  . . . school structure, conditions of work, and decision-making
  processes within schools
- changes in the distribution of power between schools and their
  clients, or in the governance structure within which schools
  operate.

> (Elmore *et al.* 1990: 11)

Conley (1993) more realistically dates the origins of restructuring from the
1990s. He indicates that, before 1990, significant change in the field had

scarcely begun: most of the activity was still at the level of academic debate on structural reform:

> Much of the restructuring movement has concerned itself with changing the structures of education rather than examining its values. However, structural changes carry with them implied moral and ethical assumptions.
>
> (Conley 1993: 43)

He continues with an examination of 'these implicit assumptions embedded in the goals of school restructuring' and details (ibid.: 43–51) 'six statements . . . gleaned from a reading of the restructuring literature', almost all in the period 1990–92.

These six statements – the headings of which are listed below – are highly relevant to the clarification of what is meant by restructuring:

1   'Essentially all students can be educated to some relatively high level of functioning.'
2   'Learning is what students can do at the conclusion of education, not simply the processes to which they have been subjected.'
3   'Education has economic utility for essentially all students and for society.'
4   'Learners participate actively in their own education in a variety of ways. Learning cannot be passive.'
5   'Education is a responsibility that extends beyond schools: parents, employers, community members have responsibilities for the education of the community's young, along with a right to be included as partners in important decisions about education.'
6   'Schools may be the only place where a sense of genuine community can be developed for young people.'

Some statements need qualification. For the first, there is a need to ascertain what is understood by 'high level of functioning'. In the USA, as in the UK, there has long been a conflict between the polarities of forces for equity and those demanding excellence. Conley argues that:

> It may be that the polar relationship between these values is no longer the only or even the primary framework that should be applied to understanding societal expectations for schooling. There is every indication that schools are now being expected to address both equity and excellence simultaneously, that schools will be expected to educate essentially all students to some relatively high level of functioning.
>
> (Conley 1993: 43–4)

There is a need for teachers to be clear about the implications of this expectation. Their own experience, at all stages of their education from primary school to university, has conditioned them to an acceptance that there must be winners and losers. It is therefore difficult for them to conceive that high levels of functioning may operate in a number of discrete domains: verbal and logical–mathematical skills, musical ability, kinaesthetic awareness, spatial recognition, interpersonal and intra-personal awareness (Gardner 1983; Gardner and Hatch 1989).

The second statement highlights the concentration in our schools, imposed largely by external forces, on the results achieved by students in classrooms and examination halls rather than demonstrable outcomes of their learning. There was, certainly in the 1970s and 1980s, a considerable growth of such demonstrations: not merely in the creative fields of school concerts, plays and journalistic enterprises, but *inter alia* in science fairs and ecology surveys, and in community work as an aspect of moral and social education. Pressure on teachers' time has in many schools much reduced these opportunities for demonstrating the practical outcomes of learning.

The injunction of the fourth statement, that 'learning cannot be passive' is supported by the view that motivation

> comes largely from the child, though the social context in which the child exists is also an important factor in determining the child's interest in learning. . . . Differences in motivation often reflect different social, economic, racial, and ethnic backgrounds. In effect, certain groups are being disenfranchised from a public education in large measure because it is very difficult for them to become motivated to do the things teachers ask in the absence of any clear reasons to do so.
>
> (Conley 1993: 48–9)

It needs to be asked whether there is any radical difference between restructuring as envisaged by Corbett in 1990 and Conley in 1993. Corbett was leading a centre in Philadelphia called Research for Better Schools. His first, brief, contribution to the literature (Corbett 1990) appears, as its title *On the Meaning of Restructuring* indicates, to be directed to a clarification of the concept of restructuring as he and his colleagues were developing it in the field, and to counter what Hopkins and Lagerweij (1996: 64) describe as the superficial attractiveness of restructuring in providing 'a useful banner under which to rally the disparate groups, especially those who know what they dislike about the current ways of organising schools'.

In a later contribution, a chapter in Kershner and Connolly (1991) which is a revisitation of his earlier writing, he makes this important statement:

> Restructuring is a conjunctive concept. That is, restructuring necessarily embodies alterations in all four aspects [rules, roles, relationships, results]. . . . Restructuring acknowledges the inherent loose coupling of educational organization and the necessity for counter balancing this natural lack of systemic unity of effort and purpose.
>
> (Corbett 1991: 22)

Conley, on the other hand, can be deemed to be a collator of good practice and, from it, to have created a 'road map', as the title of his book indicates. It is clear from reading the book as a whole that his historical and philosophical analysis of restructuring stands up well; and it is equally clear that he is not demanding that all follow a set of directions towards a specific reconstructive goal, but that he is inviting all schools to explore where they stand in relation to the variables he has assembled.

One significant difference (which will be explored in the final chapter in relation to the possible use of restructuring in England and Wales) is that Corbett believes that 'restructuring is a district-wide event; although individual buildings must alter their rules, roles, relationships and results, this is unlikely to happen effectively without school district involvement' (1991: 22).

Conley, on the other hand, makes no such judgement. His extensive writings appear to be addressed to schools, rather than to districts, and to be saying: Analyse where you are and deduce from this analysis what your immediate, middle- and long-term goals are. Use criteria to establish by what steps you will proceed to those goals. Recognise that in restructuring it is necessary to view change as an entity, even though you will have to approach your aims step by step.

Nevertheless, the fact that Corbett and Conley express their concept of restructuring in different words and ways is irrelevant. If Corbett can be regarded as the pioneer of genuine restructuring, Conley is one of the key figures in promoting the concept and creating a rationale for its use by educationalists.

Choice as a feature of restructuring

There is a strong argument in the USA for restructuring schools as *gemeinschaft* institutions, communities 'of people bound together by sentiments, shared beliefs and commitments, and feelings of kinship to one another'. Raywid uses this as one of two possible aspects of restructuring. She argues that

> a school of choice will be even more likely than a site-management school to respond to individual students and parents. The fact that

> a school is chosen alters the relationship between chooser and chosen
> in ways that school governance changes may not accomplish. It
> stands to reason that a balancing of statuses and power differences
> and a resultant mutuality are more likely to arise in a relation to
> which neither of the parties involved is assigned or remains captive.
>
> (Raywid 1990b: 169)

The value of this proposed element in restructuring needs serious consideration, not least because it was a significant feature of Conservative
government policy in England and Wales. In the USA the logical extension of decentralisation is thought by some (for example, Budde 1989) to
be 'education by charter'.

> In this method, teachers in effect become independent contractors
> within the school district. The board of education sets the proce-
> dures for establishing and evaluating educational charters, and the
> central administration provides certain services to all charters, such
> as payroll and planning. Groups of teachers petition the school
> district to sign an 'Educational Charter' that authorises the teachers
> to create and provide a complete educational program for students
> . . . within certain legal and policy parameters established by the
> school board. . . . The teacher team has complete discretion in deter-
> mining how money is spent.
>
> (Conley 1993: 234)

Some states – Minnesota and California were the first – enacted legislation
to allow both public and private schools to receive charters.
  Conley offers an even-handed view of this development:

> It remains to be seen whether the . . . experiments will lead to the
> creation of new educational environments, or will simply recreate
> isolated versions of the existing public school system. . . . There is
> an obvious danger in allowing schools to reflect different beliefs
> and values through their instructional programs. A key challenge
> will be to see whether such schools will operate within the main-
> stream of the American value system to the degree that taxpayers
> will not object to their monies going to support the education that
> takes place in those schools.
>
> (Conley 1993: 235)

There was no likelihood of charter schools being introduced on this side of
the Atlantic, since their function is far removed from anything that might
be practical within the context of our educational system. However, choice
already exists in England and Wales in a variety of ways. The Conservative

government's policy of open enrolment in the 1980s and early 1990s meant that 'parents are free to choose the school to which to send their children, and, as the children move around the system, the funding follows them' (Davies and Anderson 1992: 8). This is not, of course, a meaningful choice for many parents. In rural and suburban areas the proximity of school to home is, particularly at primary level, often an overriding consideration, and the 'chosen' school is the local school. Where choice is a possibility, and particularly in areas where there are more places available than pupils to fill them, a school's skill in marketing is a powerful and not always legitimate influence on choice. It may be that the most valuable effect of open enrolment has been to alert schools to the need for openness to what parents consider to be the desirable criteria of the good school; and this is not necessarily the school with the highest ratings in tests or examinations.

The promise of funding at levels and for purposes that the LEA would never be able to provide was obviously a significant incentive for parents to opt for grant-maintained status. Another was to prevent the reorganisation by LEAs of the relatively few selective schools that remained. Of the first 109 schools to be granted GM status, thirty-five were selective schools. The intention of the Labour government elected in 1997 was to reconstitute grant-maintained schools as 'foundation' schools, and to control the level of funding so that LEA schools are no longer disadvantaged. The second type of school that offers choice is the technology college, conceived initially as a partnership in which 'the principle of funding will be that the promoters will meet all or a substantial part of the capital costs' (DES 1986b: 8).

Choice soon took on a different meaning for these schools. Their catchment areas were, initially at least, precisely drawn, and there was an obligation on colleges to ensure that all categories of ability were represented. Parents might seek to choose a city technology college for their child at age 11, but the decision on admission rested with the college, based on an applicant's aptitude for schooling with a technological bias.

It is unlikely that, in England and Wales, the extension of choice could or would be achieved through restructuring. The experience of grant-maintained schools and city technology colleges already illustrates the impossibility of delivering total freedom of choice. If restructuring is to be an effective contribution to the improvement of all schools, then choice will be a minimal contribution to that end.

The dimensions of restructuring

At the beginning of the decade interest in the USA in restructuring was growing fast. Murphy (1991) cites in the bibliography of his book thirteen articles and professional papers, and five books or booklets, specifically addressing the issue of restructuring. Two years later Conley (1993) cites thirty articles and professional papers and twenty-five books or booklets, none of which are duplicated in Murphy's bibliography. This was a time when a number of American writers were emphasising the social and political advantages of restructuring, without giving serious attention to how it might be implemented, and relatively few were drawing attention to the processes that needed to be considered. Murphy and Conley were among these few.

> Restructuring generally encompasses systemic change in one or more of the following: work rules and organisational milieu; organisational and governance structures, including connections [between] the school and its larger environment; and core technology. Restructuring also involves fundamental alterations in the relationships among the players involved in the educational process. ... The predominant components of restructuring [are] changes in the design of work, alterations in the organisation and governance structures, and revisions to the core technology. School-based management, choice, teacher empowerment, and teaching for understanding represent the four most prevalent strategies employed in restructuring schools. Teachers as leaders, parents as partners, are the new metaphors of restructuring.
>
> (Murphy 1991: 15)

Conley agrees with Murphy's analysis, save for the phrase 'one or more'. Conley's view is holistic. He mapped what he called the component variables, all of which need the attention of those committed to restructuring if success is to be assured. He listed (1993: 106) three sets of variables, detailed in Table 3.1.

Table 3.1 Conley's variables

Central variables	Learner outcomes
	Curriculum
	Instruction
	Assessment/evaluation
Enabling variables	Learning environment
	Technology
	School/community relationships
	Time
Supporting variables	Governance
	Teacher leadership
	Personnel
	Working relationships

The following sections detail each set:

- central variables
- enabling variables
- supporting variables.

Central variables

These constitute the 'core technology of teaching' (Elmore *et al.* 1990), a phrase Murphy (1991) also uses and which, encapsulated in these four central variables, can be summed up as the learning process. Conley (1993: 107) argues thus:

> If it is possible to bring about change in these areas, then it will be possible to say that education is really experiencing fundamental change. [Yet] when developing 'restructuring' strategies, most educators appear to prefer to look first at change in almost anything other than these variables.

In England and Wales, teachers have become, understandably, so preoccupied with the demands, and the modifications to those demands, of the National Curriculum that it has become a commonplace in some schools to argue that decision making in this central area is now out of their hands. Yet, even if the National Curriculum were the distillation of all wisdom in each subject area, its delivery is still dependent on the strategies that teachers use to engage their students in the learning process. To do this they need to share with them the aims of a lesson or a series of lessons and to evaluate with them the immediate learner outcomes. Some students learn simply for the love of learning; others are compliant, but not necessarily engaged; but an increasing number demand, overtly or by their attitude to what goes on in the classroom, to know what is the point of what is being presented to them. Restructuring needs to build on this.

Assessment and evaluation must be restructured away from ranking pupil attainment towards devising and implementing strategies by which both teacher and learner examine the outcomes of the learning process. For some teachers, for whom outcomes equate with test or examination performance, whether as part of their own educational philosophy or, more probably, resulting from the institution by the DfEE of league tables of school performance, this is a variable which will cause much heart-searching. To challenge the argument that 'standards will fall' if teachers do not dominate all aspects of the learning process requires an act of faith.

Enabling variables

Conley states:

> The ability to bring about changes in the central variables often
> requires, or is closely aided by, alterations of other practices. . . .
> This is not to suggest that, in practice, schools proceed to plan for
> changes in the central variables, then consider how to modify the
> enabling variables in a way to support [such] changes. In many
> cases it appears that schools are limiting their focus to these enabling
> variables and hoping that changes here will ultimately lead to
> changes in the central variables.
>
> (Conley 1993: 108–9)

Ideally, the two sets of factors, central and enabling, should proceed in
tandem. Not all enabling factors, however, are within the control of the
teaching staff. The learning environment within the classroom for a primary
class of thirty is, for example, radically different from that for a class of
thirty-five or forty. Schools in depressed inner-city areas find the extension
of learning beyond the four walls of the classroom difficult, even impossible. In planning changes in the central variables, therefore, the realities
of enabling variables must be taken into account.

The provision of technological resources in schools in England and Wales
is growing but has not directly affected the presentation of the curriculum
as much as it might. However, the ease with which information may be
accessed by students, through CD-ROM, for example, has been a revolu-
tionary enabling factor.

Of the four enabling variables, time is generally regarded in England and
Wales as 'that which we do not have enough of'. In the USA, there is
increasing interest in restructuring the way time is used. Variations may
be approved at school board or district level, dependent only on the overriding obligation that students cover the range of subjects to the level
required for graduation. In England and Wales time is rigidly controlled
by the Education Acts. Although Knight (1989) wrote enthusiastically about
his school's experience in devising new patterns of use, claiming that
'managing school time is a fundamental decision', even modest variations,
as in some of Leicestershire's community colleges (White and Poster 1995),
are rarities. In five of the fifteen CTCs, however, a five-term year has been
adopted, with the summer break reduced to four weeks (*Guardian*, Education
Supplement, 24 June 1997); and in the same issue of the *Guardian* Anita
Higham, Principal of Banbury College, argues that 'schools and teachers
are far too valuable a resource to be left as under-used as they are'. The
main possibility for change lies in the voluntary extension of the school
day. It may be that eventually strategies for the better use of time might

evolve in our primary and secondary schools, but, in today's climate, and under present regulations, time is not an enabling variable, but a constraint on restructuring.

Schools, largely through their own concern for communicating with parents of their present and future pupils, have engaged with much success in the development of school–parent relationships. However, this is not the same as school–community relationships. For restructuring, there is a need for schools to consider all potential community partners in the educational process: shopkeepers, who may see the standards set by the school negated by a few pupils and who will often regard this as evidence of the general indiscipline of all pupils; businesses which, certainly at secondary level, can contribute to the delivery of the curriculum and aid students to an understanding of their place in the community; places of worship, particularly in multicultural areas, clubs, the medical and social services, whatever the community has to offer the school or the school has to offer the community. The need is for schools to be responsive to their external environments.

Supporting variables

Conley (1993: 110) argues that these variables

> are the furthest removed from classroom life in their immediate impact and are, paradoxically, being touted by some reformers as the prerequisites to any changes in classroom behaviors. . . . All initiatives to decentralise decision making in schools fall under the category of governance, be they site-based management, participatory management, school-based decision making, or any of the variations on this theme.

While his views about the wide diversity of practice in the USA over the relationship of these variables to the restructuring process are understandable, local management of schools in England and Wales is prescribed by legislation, and it is therefore incumbent on schools to make it work. It is difficult to conceive of restructuring – other than in a form externally imposed, the success of which is highly problematical – without a structure of decentralised decision making. The governing body has both a decision-making and a supportive role to play in the restructuring process, roles that the case studies which follow (Chapters 5–9) indicate are not well understood. The effective school leader will ensure that change is understood and endorsed by the governors. Change must also have the support of the entire school staff. This does not mean that every individual is involved in every detail. It is more important that there is trust that the restructuring process is being managed in the best interest of all.

As indicated in the previous two chapters, one of the by-products of the increased complexity of school management over the past ten years has been the growth of new leadership roles. There are of course potential dangers: these roles, if their parameters are not clearly defined and communicated to colleagues, can threaten the existing leadership structure; and roles which no longer have a valued purpose may become redundant, with those post-holders feeling a sense of grievance whatever the logic behind the change has been. Working relationships within the school depend extensively on good communication. The leadership of any school engaging in restructuring must inform, be open to suggestions for alternative ways of achieving objectives, and sometimes hold back if the time for a move forward does not seem opportune.

The view that 'most initiatives that fly the restructuring banner advocate strategies for altering power relationships' (Leithwood 1992: 8) leads to a consideration of the analogy between school restructuring and the groundshift in large-scale businesses and industries that began more than a decade ago and has rarely been perceived until recently as applicable to schools. Ouchi (1981) had differentiated between what he called type A and type Z business organisations. Leithwood (1992: 8–9) summarises the applicability of Ouchi's analysis to schools.

> [Type A organisations], very useful for some situations and tasks, centralise control and maintain differences in status between workers and management and among levels of management; they also rely on top-down decision processes. Type Z organisations emphasise participative decision making as much as possible. They are based on a radically different form of power that is consensual and facilitative in nature – a form of power manifested through other people, not over other people. . . . Facilitative power arises also as school staff members learn how to make the most of their collective capacities in solving school problems.

External monitoring and inspection

There is no mention of inspection in the key books and articles on restructuring, nor does Conley cite it as a variable: reasonably, since inspection lies outside the control of the school. While there is in the USA no national inspectorial body such as exists in England and Wales, school outcomes are rigidly monitored through standardised tests. Where there appears to be a lowering of achievement standards, the state will intervene, either of its own volition or at the behest of the school board.

In England and Wales, in contrast, there has been a long tradition of inspection, from the days of payment by results to the present role of the Office for Standards in Education (OFSTED). It is impossible to generalise the role of the LEA: although the 1944 Act gave LEAs the right to inspect their schools, many chose to work with schools in an advisory rather than inspectorial capacity (Maychell and Keys 1993). The 1992 Education Act diminished the roles of both HMI and the LEA, while OFSTED's declared purpose was initially, as expressed in its *Handbook for the Inspection of Schools* (1993: 17), to conduct 'an appraisal of the quality and standards of education in the school [with] the emphasis throughout . . . on judgements and evaluation'.

This view of OFSTED as a totally external arbiter was to undergo some alteration. Following the first inspections in Autumn 1993, the inspection framework was modified, with the result that it now requires the inspection

> to give a greater emphasis to the school's capability to manage change and review its own systems for institutional development. The inspection [is] to pay greater attention to a school's own evaluation of its strengths and weaknesses. . . . Schools [are] expected to monitor and evaluate their performance, systematically and regularly.
>
> (Earley *et al.* 1996: 11)

One would like to believe that this considerable change of approach is a result of a growing recognition that the self-managing school is becoming increasingly skilled in the process of evaluation.

The growth and diversification of restructuring

In their book entitled *Restructuring Schools* Elmore *et al.* (1990: 292) observe:

> One of the key insights behind restructuring is the idea that overall improvement of American education depends on getting individual schools to operate more effectively as institutions. Those who propose school restructuring have a bias toward changing the system by changing individual schools; according to them, systemwide change will occur by lodging greater responsibility with people who work in schools.
>
> (ibid.: 292)

It is clear from the early literature that the impetus for restructuring initially came from school districts rather than from individual schools:

> We began with a telephone survey of over a hundred districts to locate those that best represented districts whose actions have led to new roles and relationships and organisational arrangements. We

selected three districts for more intensive study. . . . These districts are by no means the only ones undergoing significant change . . .

(David 1990: 211)

David continues by citing published accounts of districts in California, Ohio, New York City, Indiana and New York State. At the same time, it appears, a significant number of states were promoting school reform, though these initiatives were almost certainly with selected schools or districts, not state-wide. Furthermore, reform policies vary from state to state, and within districts in the same state.

> A 1989 survey by the American Governors' Association indicated that thirty states had adopted or were implementing state-level initiatives to promote school reform. Additional reform efforts are being generated at the local school-district level.
>
> (Koppich and Guthrie 1993: 57)

In Europe, and more particularly in those countries which were formerly in the Communist bloc, there is a stronger case for a national approach to restructuring in education since it is arguably linked with political transformation. The fundamental changes that are taking place in education in countries such as Poland are recognisably derivative from and supportive of the political, economic and societal changes that are taking place concurrently.

It may well prove to be immaterial that restructuring initiatives are wholly school based, as they are as yet in England and Wales, district- or state-based as in the USA, or national as in Poland, Romania and other countries formerly in the Communist bloc. It is the concept and the processes required to realise that concept that matter. Restructuring is not a nostrum but a means whereby schools, whether of their own initiative or through the encouragement of their LEAs, can visualise a holistic structure for continuous improvement. To be successful it needs to be a way of life within the individual school and not a one-off attempt to remedy the present deficiencies of educational systems worldwide. It is therefore essential that the long-term view that is implicit in futures approaches is absorbed into every aspect of the school's work. Furthermore, these futures approaches must influence the governance of schools, in particular because now there exists the potential under school-based management to devise new structures and strategies both to meet present-day needs and to plan for future developments.

The next chapter will set out the methodology which was adopted in the case studies which follow in Chapters 5–9.

4

CHOOSING THE APPROPRIATE
RESEARCH METHODOLOGY

Introduction

This book describes an investigation into the extent to which a sample of schools can be determined as having restructured their curriculum delivery and management procedures to have become more effective schools: it is therefore interpretive and subjective. The previous chapter sought to demonstrate that restructuring is not a theory, but a process. I have attempted, therefore, to construct a methodology through which the managerial and organisational effectiveness of a school can be examined. There is no 'perfect fit'; nor is there a best way in which restructuring can be achieved. Restructuring begins by investigating what a school has achieved in order to attain its present status and what it plans to do to maintain and improve upon it.

My intention was, as a first step, to confirm the expectation that the case study schools (covered in Chapters 5–9) are indeed effective schools, and, importantly, that their policies and development plans are understood by staff at all levels. For the former purpose, I measured the data from interviews with, in particular, the headteacher and from the school's documentation against the effectiveness criteria established by Mortimore (1993). For the latter, interviews with staff were conducted using the framework of the Stages of Concern (SoC) element of the long-established Concerns-based Adoption Model (CBAM), developed in the USA from 1973 and now in use in a number of countries (details of this model appear in Figure 4.2).

The second stage of the case study research was to analyse the extent to which these five schools can be regarded as restructuring schools. For this purpose the writings of Corbett (1990) and Conley (1993), referred to in Chapter 3, were used extensively as a baseline for determining this hypothesis. This analysis is undertaken in Chapter 10.

The case study approach required, in addition to interviews and the study of supporting documentation, a choice between the 'two principal types of observation – participant observation and non-participant observation'

(Conley 1993: 107). Had the subject of this research been a limited topic, for example a specific aspect of restructuring such as improved classroom performance following a major change in teaching strategies and learning styles, then either type of observation might have been used. However, the purpose of these case studies was one of enquiry, over months rather than weeks, into what organisational and managerial strategies have been used to attain certain ends for the school as a whole.

Applying Conley's dimensions of restructuring

Conley's dimensions of restructuring, described in the previous chapter (pp. 45–50), are appropriate for use within this research programme, with the proviso that there are differences, some significant, between the educational culture and practices of the two nations. It is necessary, for example, to view the central variables in particular from the context of the centralised–decentralised dichotomy of the present control of our schools. Thus the National Curriculum imposes a high level of centralised control on the curriculum in England and Wales, enforced by the Key Stage attainment targets. The extent to which this may impede restructuring is considered in Chapter 11 (see pp. 167–72).

The differing interpretation, on the two sides of the Atlantic, of time as an enabling factor was referred to in the previous chapter. Other enabling factors are equally applicable to restructuring in England and Wales. Educationalists in the USA may have different interpretations of the supporting variables, but in England and Wales there should be no difficulty in adopting the principles of these variables and adapting them to local circumstances.

Choosing the case study schools

A random sample of schools was unlikely to serve the purpose of this enquiry; an unmanageably large sample would have been required to find out what proportion of schools were engaged in restructuring and at what level. In any case, a quantitative survey was not the purpose of this research. Schools were selected on the basis of prior knowledge. The schools were at different stages of development, but there was a strong expectation of finding a sound understanding of how to adapt to change. The five case studies are of an infants school, two primary schools, and two secondary schools – one 11–16 and the other 13–18.

The concerns-based approach

Restructuring would be seriously impeded if there were a gap between the perception of a change model by the school leadership and its application by the staff. There is, fortunately, a long-established and well-tried approach to identify any such gap, originating in the USA and used since in many countries. I was trained in this evaluation strategy in 1983, and have used it extensively since.

The Research and Development Center for Teacher Education at the University of Texas at Austin was a pioneer in developing a research methodology for the study of change in schools. The Concerns-based Adoption Model (CBAM) is 'an empirically-based conceptual framework which outlines the developmental process that individuals experience as they implement an innovation' (Hall *et al.* 1973). It rests on seven basic assumptions about change and how it is best facilitated:

- *Change is a process, not an event* The recognition that this process takes place, almost invariably, over a period of years is essential to its successful implementation.
- *Change is made by individuals first* Only when a change process has been accepted and implemented by a sufficient number of individuals can it be said that the institution to which they belong has changed.
- *Change is a highly personal experience* Participants in the change process react differently and failure to recognise those differences will inhibit the progress of initiation and assimilation of change.
- *Change entails multilevel development growth* Even within an individual, change is not a totally coherent, rational, unitary function. Rather, what we label 'change' is an irregular assemblage of emotional, intellectual and behavioural responses that affect the individual and thus the school in a variety of ways.
- *Change is best understood in operational terms* Teachers relate to change in terms of what it means to their practice within the classroom or to their involvement in or response to the management of the school.
- *Change facilitation must suit individual needs* CBAM is a 'client-centred' diagnostic model which can identify the requirements of an individual at that point in time and enable the change facilitator to take appropriate action where needs for discussion, training or modification are perceived.
- *Change efforts should focus on individuals, not innovations* The innovation package does not of itself effect change; only people can make change by altering their behaviour.

(Hord 1987: 93–6; abbreviated)

There are three components of CBAM: Levels of Use, Stages of Concern and Innovation Configurations. In this study we are dealing with restructuring; that is, whole-school change, and not with change specific to one area of potential development, a curricular innovation, for example. In CBAM the Innovation Configuration posits a checklist under as many head-ings as seem appropriate to the innovation, and then categorises teacher response as ideal – that is, that they accord with the change model that has been established and agreed – as *acceptable*, and as *unacceptable*. In an example provided by Hord (1987: 123), the checklist of an innovatory primary mathematics programme has six components, two of which were materials–equipment and diagnosis. For these components, definitions had been agreed and are as shown in Table 4.1.

It is obvious that a configuration devised primarily for curriculum inno-vation does not easily lend itself to use for whole-school change and the complexity entailed. Furthermore, while the standards of acceptability are, in the example given, those determined by the curriculum developers and agreed by the innovating school, quantification, explicit or implicit, has no place in the current study. Since the purpose of the research is to identify the features that, taken together, both characterise the successful school and indicate that restructuring is taking place in order to achieve that success, it therefore seems reasonable to use only positive or 'ideal' indicators.

Indicators appropriate to this research, drawing extensively on the work of Mortimore (1993), were defined by the National Commission on Education (1993: 142–3), and used in the major case study research which followed (1996). While an effective school is not necessarily a restructur-ing school, a school which demonstrates its commitment to the restruc-turing process is likely to show a positive response to all or most of these indicators. Key-words from these indicators were used to compile a check-list to ensure that the initial interviews and the study of the school's documentation had covered all areas relevant to the effectiveness of the school. The same indicators were also presented in the form of a questionnaire

Table 4.1 Example of an innovation configuration checklist

Ideal	*Acceptable*	*Unacceptable*
At least five different programme materials are used with each child each session	At least three different programme materials are used with each child each session	Fewer than three different programme materials are used with each child each session
Children are diagnosed individually using a combination of tests and teacher judgement	Children are diagnosed individually using teacher judgement only	Children are not diagnosed individually

Source: Hord 1987

to governors asking for responses in terms of: 'very true', 'true' and 'not true of the school' at this time.

Levels of Use (LoU) focuses on behaviours and skills relative to an inno-vation, while Stages of Concern (SoC) 'represents the affective dimension of change; that is, how it is perceived by individuals' (Hord 1987: 109). LoU is interview-based, and the responses classify respondents under eight cate-gories, each with a behavioural index of level (see Table 4.2). LoU is appropriate for establishing the extent to which teachers have taken on board a curriculum development or a new procedure. The problem in using LoU to determine individual use of a multi-dimensional change is that the complexity of the innovation does not lend itself to this kind of classifica-tion. For specific aspects of the restructuring process within the school development plan it would certainly be possible to identify levels of use by individual staff: the introduction of a school policy to establish within each classroom an agreed list of what constitutes acceptable pupil behav-iour, for example. From its use in such a situation, the senior management team might well gain valuable insights into the relationship between policy and practice. Restructuring is, however, concerned with holistic change. While it is the individual who delivers those elements of the change appro-priate to her/him, and who needs to comprehend the change as a whole, even when an element is the direct concern of someone else, the change process is not subject to fragmentation. Consequently LoU is in this respect an inappropriate evaluation tool.

Stages of Concern (SoC), on the other hand, is both appropriate and valu-able as an evaluation instrument:

> [It] may be aptly characterised as the cornerstone of the whole CBAM model. In theory, SoC is a fundamental conceptual tool for

Table 4.2   Levels of Use

Level of Use	Behavioural indices of level
6 Renewal	The user is seeking more effective alternatives to the established use of the innovation
5 Integration	The user is making deliberate efforts to coordinate with others in using the innovation
4b Refinement	The user is making changes to increase outcomes
4a Routine	The user is making few or no changes and has an established pattern of use
3 Mechanical use	The user is making changes to organise better use of the innovation
2 Preparation	The individual is preparing to use the innovation
1 Orientation	The individual is seeking information about the innovation
0 Non-use	No action is being taken with respect to the innovation

approaching innovation of whatever sort; in practice it is a valuable technique for information gathering and for formative evaluation of innovative use. In fact, all of the CBAM-related work on assessing and facilitating the innovation process, and thus the promotion of productive, positive and lasting change, is firmly grounded in the theory and practice of SoC.

(Hord 1987: 97)

The seven elements of SoC and typical 'longhand' interpretations of what that stage implies are demonstrated in Table 4.3. If there were wider use of SoC in this country there would be merit in a review of the model. Fortunately, there are within the present design of CBAM two other acceptable ways of collecting information about an individual's concerns, which can then form the basis for making assessments. The first is the open-ended statement in which respondents are asked to summarise their concerns about a particular innovation. The interviewer uses the statement to code into the Stages of Concern the level indicated by the recorded responses. While this has the advantage that the interview is non-directive, its disadvantage lies in the degree of responsibility placed on the interviewer to make an accurate interpretation of the responses. For the research reported in this book, it is doubtful whether this procedure would have provided data as reliable as those from the alternative procedure.

The second way is that which is common to all the interviews in these case studies: the focused interview. Because it is conducted orally, informally and face-to-face, it is generally regarded by respondents as less threatening than the questionnaire and more personalised than the open-ended statement. The skilled author is able to maintain the focus without inhibiting the expression of the respondent's opinions and concerns. It is possible to tape-record these interviews, but this is in itself inhibiting to many interviewees, and 'key-wording' during the interview is usually sufficient to enable the experienced researcher to assess the respondent's

Table 4.3 Typical expressions of concern about the innovation

Stages of concern	Expressions of concern
6 Refocusing	I have some ideas about what would work even better.
5 Collaboration	I am concerned about relating what I am doing with what other teachers are doing.
4 Consequence	How is my use affecting students?
3 Management	I seem to be spending all my time getting materials ready.
2 Personal	How will using it affect me?
1 Informational	I would like to know more about it.
0 Awareness	I am not concerned about the innovation.

stages of concern. However, the interviewer is able to double-check: the interviewee is asked at the end of the discussion of each of the Stages of Concern to estimate independently on the grid (Figure 4.1) where she/he stands in each of the seven areas (0–6), and the researcher compares this with the estimate that she/he has made. If a significant difference is found, then further discussion is needed to reconcile the two views.

For this alternative to the questionnaire, a much simpler assessment of the elements of the Stages of Concern is used. This consists of a grid of three levels of concern – high, medium and low – each subdivided into three, giving nine sections, plus a tenth for use on those rare occasions when the respondent makes a case for 'no concern at all' (see Figure 4.1). Hatching gives a visual presentation of the relationship between the stages, without the unnecessary precision of a graph of percentile points.

The focused interview provides incidental content-related information not available from the questionnaire. That the results of SoC have been presented in histogram form does not prevent them from being usefully compared with the hypothesised development of Stages of Concern (Hord 1987: 107). The three SoC profiles relevant to these case studies, those of the inexperienced user, the experienced user and the renewing user, have been 'translated' from Hord's percentile curves into the histograms that appear in Figure 4.2. Comparisons with the histograms of those interviewed (which appear in the case studies) are thus easier to make.

Hord's checklist (Table 4.1) was constructed to depict typical profiles corresponding to the changes in a single user over a period of time, but is of no less value in providing a template against which to place the results

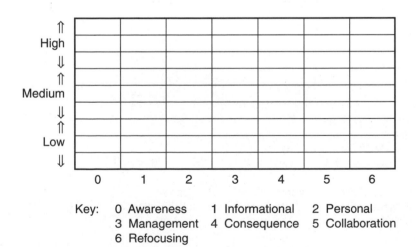

Key: 0 Awareness   1 Informational   2 Personal
       3 Management   4 Consequence   5 Collaboration
       6 Refocusing

Figure 4.1   The histogram grid

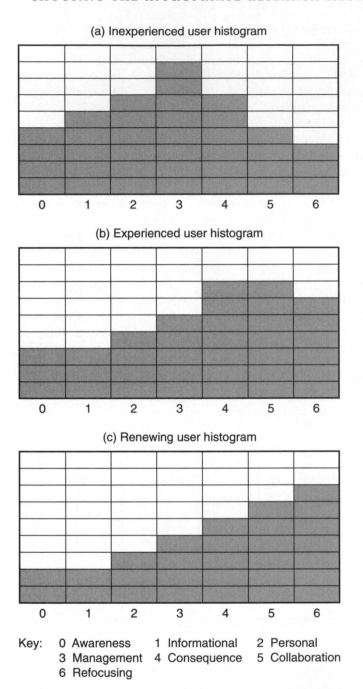

Figure 4.2 Hypothesised development of SoCs for inexperienced, experienced and renewing users

of a number of interviews conducted at the same time within the one school. Hord (1987: 94) offers sound advice in interpretation that comes from extensive use of CBAM.

- Nonusers of an innovation are high in intensity on stages 0, 1 and 2.
- New and inexperienced users show a sharp elevation of management concerns [1, 2, 3].
- Experienced users . . . are more likely to have reduced informational, personal and management concerns; and, if the appropriate support and facilitative interventions have been taken, consequence and collaboration concerns may start to predominate [4 and 5].
- Finally, refocusing users, by virtue of experience, show very low stage 0–2 concerns, low management concerns, and intense stage 6 concerns. These are . . . the 'better mousetrap builders', who are always in search of ways to make improvements.

Interviewing the headteacher

The two main purposes of the headteacher interview were for the author to

1 learn about the development of school policy from the beginning of the headteacher's incumbency; and
2 gain an understanding of how each area of the school development plan might be identified as features of a restructuring school.

The school development plans, past and present, were key data. The initial interview with the headteacher set out to determine what the headteacher considered to be the salient features of these plans, how far they had been realised, and what remained to be done in the foreseeable future. In some cases the current plan had been made available before this interview; in other cases it and relevant previous plans were provided as part of the documentation to supplement the discussion. Headteachers were encouraged to speak freely about their plans and aspirations for future development, and difficulties they had encountered. The main task was to ensure, by prompting, that all areas had been covered, and after the interview to transcribe interview notes into a continuous text, which was later shared with the headteacher to ensure that it accurately reflected his/her views.

In a subsequent interview the checklist provided a framework for ensuring that all areas relevant to an examination of restructuring were covered. In view of the considerable amount of information and data that had to be obtained in a relatively short time, the checklist proved to be an essential research tool.

Interviewing staff

With school staff, the more specific interview schedule set out, first, to discover the extent of teacher awareness of the change processes in which the school was engaged and, second, to introduce and clarify the purpose of the Stages of Concern (SoC) of the Concerns-based Adoption Model (CBAM). CBAM is widely used in the USA as an instrument for establishing the effectiveness of restructuring, either alone or, more frequently, as one of a battery of evaluative techniques, as in the extensive programme Washington State Schools for the Twenty-first Century (Anderson 1993). Conley cites *Taking Charge of Change* (Hord *et al.* 1987) to stress the importance of CBAM in the evaluation of restructuring.

Researchers are well aware that what headteachers and senior management teams may understand to be school policy is by no means as well understood by others. Those outside the normal decision-making structures may have concerns about, for example, lack of information, or the implications for their classroom management of decisions taken at a higher level. It is for this reason that this set of staff interviews was planned, to determine what the interviewees' levels of concern were in the seven key stages from awareness to refocusing described in Table 4.3.

The overall intention of the headteacher interview coupled with the staff interviews was to ascertain the extent to which the school had adapted to the management demands of the 1990s, and, in particular, had recognised, implicitly or explicitly, the processes involved in meeting these demands. Observation during visits, school publications and outcomes' data available in the main from Key Stage test results and, for secondary schools, examination results, were to provide supportive information.

The scattergram

In addition to the individual SoC profiles that arose from the interviews, I was of the opinion that consolidation in a scattergram of the seven SoC elements of those interviewed in each school would provide useful evidence. The scattergram was constructed by transferring the profiles onto a histogram grid (Figure 4.1). For each of those interviewed the seven elements are then indicated by asterisks in the appropriate vertical box in each column.

The focused interview

Merton and Kendall (1946) pointed out that the focused interview requires interviewer control of the kinds of question used and so to limit the discussion to certain parts of the respondent's experience. They identified four ways in which the focused interview differed from other types of research interview:

1   the persons interviewed are known to have been involved in a particular situation;
2   by means of the techniques of content analysis elements of the situation which the researcher deems significant have previously been analysed;
3   using the analysis as a basis, the investigator constructs an interview guide;
4   the actual interview is focused on the subjective experiences of the people who have been exposed to the situation.

The structure of the SoC interview is largely predetermined, but nevertheless the interviewer needs to be sure that the interviews meet these criteria and that the responses are, as far as possible, without bias.

Summary of the research stages

It was necessary, first, to ascertain, as pointed out in the introduction to this chapter, that the case study schools, chosen because they were believed to be effective schools, were indeed so. An effective school will not necessarily be effective in every aspect of its planned development, but it must demonstrate that it is well led, has a deep concern for 'the core technology of learning', and that staff are supportive of the school's programme for improvement. The interviews and the data search were intended initially to confirm that these five schools, whatever their differences in stage of development or response to the age group which they serve, are indeed effective schools. Each case study therefore concludes with an analysis of criteria to this end.

Given that they qualify in this respect, the next stage is to analyse the extent to which the five schools collectively can be classed as restructuring schools. Here, too, differences will be observed. Restructuring is a continuous process and covers a wide range of variables not all of which can be pursued at the same time. What is important is that the schools, individually and collectively, show an awareness both of what they have achieved towards restructuring and of what will be the direction of future developments.

5

WEST TOWN LANE
INFANTS SCHOOL

Introduction

This is an infants school with 180 on roll in two parallel classes in each of the three years: Reception, Year 1, Year 2. The present headteacher took up her post in January 1993, having been deputy head there since May 1990. The latter role was imprecisely defined, with no formal job description, and her only clearly defined activity was responsibility for the curriculum. Her predecessor was the last in the LEA to accept local management of schools (LMS) and it was left to the new incumbent to introduce local financial management (LFM) the year after her appointment. She stated that she had inherited a remarkably high figure of unspent funds, about which the staff and the governors knew nothing.

There are eight assistant teachers, including two pairs involved in job-sharing. Only two were appointed before or at the same time as the headteacher arrived as deputy: six, three full-time and three job-sharing, were appointed on her recommendation to governors.

Because this school was the first of the five case study schools to be visited, a return visit was made eighteen months later, at the end of 1996. Developments that had taken place in the interim appear in the relevant sections. In addition, since the school was temporarily without a deputy when initial visits were made, the new deputy, in post for four terms, was interviewed on the return visit.

Developments in organisation and management

One of the first tasks of the new incumbent was to create a pattern of management appropriate to her future aspirations for the school. Within a short time she had set up a senior management team, established a pattern of staff meetings that ensured that communication was both vertical and horizontal, and introduced significant changes and developments. In 1996 the senior management team was reorganised and is now entitled, simply, 'the management team'. It consisted of the headteacher and deputy, all

64

full-time members of staff except a newly qualified teacher, and one representative of the four job-share teachers.

Staff

All staff have areas of responsibility which have been allocated through
negotiation. Senior staff perform defined management tasks, the evaluation
of which is part of their biennial appraisal. All staff are consulted about
major decisions, though the headteacher clearly retains overall responsibility
for decision making. The former deputy had a defined role as curriculum
leader, but when the new deputy was appointed in 1996 roles were revised
since curriculum coordinators no longer appeared to need detailed monitoring. The headteacher therefore continues to oversee all curriculum
development and, for the new incumbent, the deputy's role was reconsti-
tuted as that of curriculum moderator. There was still, as can be seen from
the next section, whole-school planning of curriculum development. The
budget had been planned to allow for non-pupil contact time for all staff,
including the school secretary, with agreed personal plans for appropriate
activities in that time.

School development plan

The senior management team, together with any other staff who were
interested, had worked with governors to draw up the mission statement:
'[The school] is committed to preserving and expanding its aims for a caring
environment where all are enabled to develop and fulfil their whole potential.' That this was a corporate activity has been a significant means of
drawing together headteacher, governors and staff.

The first school development plan was drawn up in 1993 by the present
headteacher shortly after her appointment, and the five-year rolling
programme is reviewed with staff at an INSET day at the end of each school
year. At this review meeting the programme for the next year is worked
out in detail. For 1995–96, for example, there were nine targets, most of
them revising aspects of existing policies, but some opening up areas in
which written policies did not yet exist. As an example, target 2 focused
on quality teaching and learning. The target sheet is drawn up under seven
heads. The first of these is the goal: 'to deliver a quality teaching and
learning environment for all the children in our school'. This is followed
by the target, immediate and long-term; purposes; needs analysis; action
to be taken by a set date with the staff responsibility for implementation
assigned; success criteria; and review procedure. This is the standard format
for each element of the school development plan review.

There are sixteen policies concerned with learning and teaching, nine
of them subject-specific, the remaining seven concerned with whole-school

policy areas, such as self-esteem, behaviour and special educational needs. In addition there are twenty non-curricular policies that form a valuable handbook for staff and governors and that include key areas such as the induction of new pupils, parental involvement, staffing policy, assessment and records. In addition, there are practical guidelines, for example on school excursions. There is a cost–benefit analysis as part of the review.

No element of this holistic concept of management existed in the school before the appointment of the present headteacher. Nor were governors previously presented with the policies and policy revisions for their approval as they were created, even though they have had responsibility for school policy since the Education Act (No. 2) of 1986. Both staff and governors express their enthusiasm for the thoroughness of the policy statements and for their involvement in their creation and revision.

A key element of the development plan was that core-subject coordinators are responsible for setting up and reviewing subject policy and practice within the framework of the agreed school development plan. In 1996 schemes of work were superseded by a curriculum map, the relevant section of which is developed and overseen by each coordinator. The crucial role of the headteacher is to ensure their synthesis into a whole-school curriculum policy. Special needs was an area of concern for all staff.

Different learning/teaching styles for pupils of different abilities and aptitudes are encouraged. To promote quality control a school portfolio has been created with examples of work appropriate to the National Curriculum levels representative of low, middle and high achievement at Key Stage 1. In addition, four children are targeted in each class throughout each area of the Key Stage and their work studied to determine both the successful implementation of the units and the steady improvement of performance of the sample. There is also a photographic record of pupils' work. To avoid overlap in topic work as pupils progress through the school, details are placed in a topic file for any member of staff to consult. During staff meetings staff engage in moderation exercises to agree standards.

The headteacher sees the planning file of each member of staff, which contains a review of the previous week and the plan for the current week, and is able to set this against the term plan for that class and the specific targets of the National Curriculum.

Pupil behaviour

'Circle time' has been introduced as a class-based weekly activity in which positive happenings are shared. Behavioural issues are dealt with in a non-authoritarian and non-threatening way. This is part of the policy of raising pupil self-esteem.

Good work and good behaviour are given equal value. There is a detailed policy on pupil behaviour for the implementation of which all staff are responsible. Class teachers are responsible for setting up, with their pupils, behavioural standards within the classroom. For outside the classroom, behavioural standards are set and maintained by the staff as a whole. Sanctions exist, but these are for remediation, not primarily to punish.

Much attention has been paid to raising the esteem in which the supervisory work in the playground of the school meal assistants (SMAs) is held. They are now less dependent on the exercise of authority and are supported by the provision of games equipment for use at their choice. Their approach is towards positive behavioural attitudes and inventiveness, for example on wet days.

The headteacher has weekly contact with all six classes, for three-quarters of an hour with Years 1 and 2, and by assisting the Reception teachers on 'reading afternoons'.

Governors

Having formerly had a very restricted and formal role, governors have now been inducted into their new responsibilities under the Education Acts. They are increasingly involved in the curriculum, receiving a report at each meeting of the governing body from a curriculum coordinator and, from the headteacher, routine reports on the development of whole-school policies. Some of these they have been directly involved in formulating, for example, the legal requirements of sex education and religious education, and behaviour. Each is assigned a class to visit in the interim between their twice-termly meetings and some have whole-school subject-specific interests. In 1996 a fourfold committee structure was set up for curriculum, personnel, finance and buildings, and grievances. This has given each governor a further personal interest in the school and, at the same time, has provided the headteacher with a small body with which to share detailed planning. For the governing body as a whole the value of the development lies in their ability to hear and approve reports from committees, where necessary, but to spend more time on whole-school issues.

There are social evenings for staff and governors, and governors have been invited on occasions when the school has hosted LEA courses and activities in the evening. There is still an expressed need for further training, and for induction programmes for new governors.

Parental and community support, and inter-school liaison

Parents are encouraged to take responsibility for their child's behaviour, through school–home contracts. There is a parental support group primarily for fund-raising, and considerable support is given by parents to the annual summer playschools. Parents have been increasingly involved in work groups, cataloguing and repairing books, and assisting with school events. An annual 'work-along' for parents and children was instituted in 1995. A mathematics work-along, for parents to gain an insight into the requirements of the National Curriculum, teaching methodology and the support they can give towards the achievement of high standards, was so well attended that it overflowed the hall into several classrooms. The 1996 half-day work-along was for science. Sixty parents signed up to come with the children, and in the event 120 turned up. Working parents are supported by a before-school (breakfast) class and an after-school class. Parents assist in classes.

Stages of Concern interviews

Five of the eight assistant members of staff were interviewed, and two ancillary members of staff, one of whom was a parent governor.

Anne: beginning teacher

At the time of the interview Anne was in her second year as a teacher. She had been appointed on the strength of an excellent performance in her final teaching practice at the school. Not surprisingly, as a beginning teacher, her profile shows some concern in the categories of awareness and information.

> [The headteacher] is an excellent communicator. We have a weekly information session before school, minutes of meetings are made available and she is ready at all times to talk with staff. I think my concern is really more with the culture shock of what I need to be aware of if I am to keep up with all aspects of school policy and activity. The fact that I did my final teaching practice at this school is a great help. Someone coming in without this advantage might find it more of a problem.

In general Anne's profile is very similar to those of other staff. Consequences are seen clearly as essentially pupil-centred: 'All our developments are aimed in the end at improving the performance of our pupils, aren't they?'

In relating her work to that of others – collaboration – she demonstrated a reasonably high concern in her relationship with the job-share teachers of the other Reception class, but understandably, at this stage of her professional development, less with teachers of other years.

There is one concern which is atypical of the inexperienced user, however: the indication of high concern with refocusing (see Figure 5.1). Already regarded by her colleagues as a teacher of high ability, a peer and not a beginner, Anne was clearly more alive to the possibilities of development under restructuring than any other member of staff interviewed. Her ideas

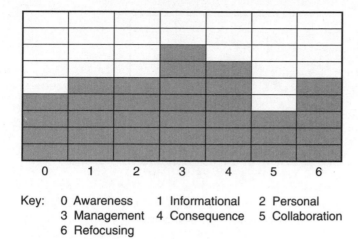

Key: 0 Awareness   1 Informational   2 Personal
       3 Management   4 Consequence   5 Collaboration
       6 Refocusing

Figure 5.1   Anne: second year of teaching

for refocusing were expressed with some diffidence, as befitted the youngest and least experienced member of staff, but they were evident and positive.

> We are a small school. In a large school I can see the value of a senior management team making decisions and communicating them to staff, but I wonder whether there might not be times when the team meeting might not be open to other staff, especially when there is a matter which is likely to be of particular interest to one or more of us. We could be observers; I would not expect us to be decision makers!

It is worthy of note that the headteacher, who had not seen the comments made at interview by any staff members, has since expanded the management team.

Beth: experienced teacher

Although an experienced teacher, Beth presented a profile more typical of the inexperienced user. This was not unexpected. Having been a full-time teacher, after a period of maternity leave she had opted for a job-sharing post. Inevitably, her involvement in the change process had diminished. She showed a higher concern about awareness than others, Anne excepted:

> It is to be expected, I suppose, but so much seems to have happened while I was away and still to be happening that I feel somewhat out of things. I will say this though. I know a lot more about the

69

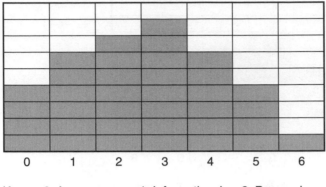

Key: 0 Awareness   1 Informational   2 Personal
       3 Management 4 Consequence   5 Collaboration
       6 Refocusing

Figure 5.2   Beth: experienced class teacher

school's aims and policies than I did under [the previous head-teacher].

Her relatively low concern about collaboration (see Figure 5.2) was very likely a sign of her disengagement as a part-time teacher from full involvement, though her commitment to her teaching was unchanged: 'I collaborate with my job-sharer about who does what in the lesson planning, and this I find very satisfying.' It may well be that, when her child is older, she will have more time for professional involvement with her colleagues.

Celia: experienced teacher

Celia is a teacher with some twenty years' experience in primary schools, and was appointed to the school at the same time as the present head-teacher was appointed deputy headteacher. On the latter's elevation, having shared with her the frustrations of unilateral management, Celia was closest to her in thinking about the way in which the school must develop in order to meet the demands of the 1990s.

> Knowing what is going on has made a considerable difference to my attitude to the school and to my teaching. All those frustrations about wondering what [the previous headteacher] was going to do or not do are gone. I feel involved at all levels. In some ways I feel under more pressure, but it is easier to take when you can see the results of the style of management [the headteacher] adopts.

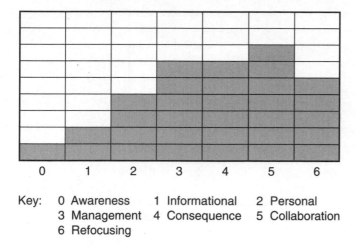

Key: 0 Awareness 1 Informational 2 Personal
      3 Management 4 Consequence 5 Collaboration
      6 Refocusing

Figure 5.3 Celia: class teacher with 20 years' experience

Her low concerns about awareness and information (see Figure 5.3), lower in these two categories than in the profiles of any other member of staff, are a reflection of the interest she has taken in the development of all aspects of management in the school over the past four years. She is regarded by the headteacher, and rightly regards herself, as a mainstay of the school, both because of her previous experience and in her involvement in the senior management team.

Diane: experienced teacher

Diane, also an experienced teacher, declared a surprisingly high level of concern in awareness and information (Figure 5.4) that were related, she felt, to her difficulties in coping with the heavy management-related demands being made on her. Her collaboration with other members of staff was lower than might be expected in a small school where much recent activity in curriculum planning must inevitably have brought her into considerable professional contact with other staff. She expressed a particular concern about the rate of change: that the policy on behaviour, for example, had possibly been developed too rapidly:

> We knew that, in the old days, we could send a child who was misbehaving to the headteacher. Sometimes all that was needed was a sharp word or two. I think we may be going too fast in a number of directions.

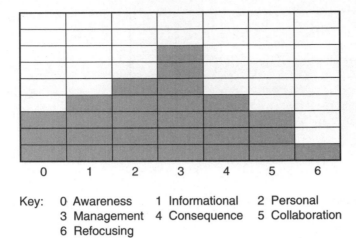

Key: 0 Awareness   1 Informational   2 Personal
      3 Management   4 Consequence   5 Collaboration
      6 Refocusing

Figure 5.4   Diane: experienced teacher

She nevertheless acknowledged that there was full support from the head-teacher in such cases, initially in helping staff to decide what action to take, and, if the misdemeanour warranted it, sending for the parent to plan remedial measures.

Ena: school secretary

The headteacher's request that the school secretary should be one of those interviewed reflected her view that the staff is defined as all those who work in the school, and therefore includes all ancillaries. Although the shape of the curve is, in general, that of the inexperienced user, it is noteworthy that Ena has somewhat atypical awareness and informational concerns, lower than might be expected (Figure 5.5). Similarly there was a high level of concern for consequence, an understanding that her role was important for the pupils' welbeing no less than as aide to the headteacher. She expressed herself as well aware of her role in the change process, and regarded it as a matter of pride that she was treated as a valued facilitator for the teaching staff.

> It is good that I am in the picture about most of what happens here because I am the first port of call for parents and visitors. So I do not feel that all I have to do is say 'I will see if the head-teacher is free'. I can often prepare the ground a little, without feeling that I am interfering. Through knowing about the school policy I can handle telephone calls better than [under the previous headteacher] because I know I am allowed to put the caller in touch with the right person, not necessarily the headteacher.

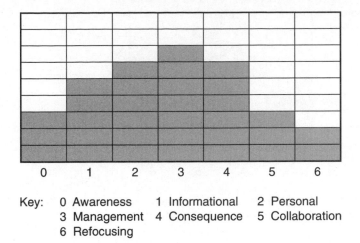

Key:　0 Awareness　　1 Informational　　2 Personal
　　　3 Management　　4 Consequence　　5 Collaboration
　　　6 Refocusing

Figure 5.5　Ena: school secretary

Management concerns are high, because of the workload, she felt, rather than from any sense of being unable to cope: 'I often feel like a circus juggler, but I don't think I fail to keep the plates spinning!'

Frances: deputy headteacher

Frances, the deputy head, had been almost four terms in post at the time of the second visit. Her first teaching post had been in a Reception-to-Year 3 school with quiet and well-behaved children, uniformly committed to learning. She had worked under an experienced headteacher, highly organised and clearly one to recognise merit, since Frances was offered a promotion point to be responsible for computer-aided design and technology (CDT) after two years. However, she had felt that she needed a more challenging experience, and had moved to a Bristol school where there were many learning and behavioural problems, to take up a post of responsibility for special needs. She had left that school on maternity leave and, when she was ready to resume teaching, applied for the post of deputy headteacher at West Town Lane.

> When I visited the school and spoke with the headteacher I felt immediately that this was the school for me. I was much impressed by what I understood had evolved in so short a time and by the commitment of the entire staff.

Her teaching role is with one of the two Year 1 classes, and she regards setting an example by aiming for the highest possible standards as a key

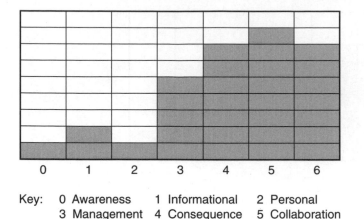

Key: 0 Awareness   1 Informational   2 Personal
       3 Management   4 Consequence   5 Collaboration
       6 Refocusing

Figure 5.6   Frances: deputy headteacher

element of her position. Her own good practice, she believes, is an incentive and encouragement to the staff as a whole. As year coordinator she has an exemplary relationship with the newly qualified member of staff who is her peer teacher. Her role as school-based evaluator gave her immediate access to the rest of the staff, and she was soon accepted by them.

> Initially it was not easy for them to see that my role was not that of adjudicator but rather someone aiming to help each of them to achieve the highest possible standard of attainment for their pupils. I think that my belief in children and my respect for the abilities of the staff were what won their support for me.

Staff management is, she believes, at the core of her role (see Figure 5.6). She finds it easy to contribute to this, largely because of what she regards as the headteacher's boundless energy and her understanding of the whole field of management. She has been impressed by the strength of parental support, sadly not evident in her previous school, though not for want of trying. The role of governors, too, she finds impressive, and she has seen them all gain in confidence and ability.

Helen: parent governor and part-time assistant

The final interview was with a parent governor who had been appointed a part-time general assistant for small groups of children with special needs. The interview reflected her main role, though it became obvious that her low awareness, informational and personal concerns (Figure 5.7) were

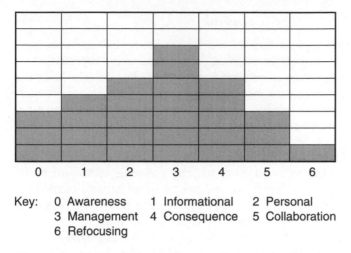

Key: 0 Awareness   1 Informational   2 Personal
        3 Management   4 Consequence   5 Collaboration
        6 Refocusing

Figure 5.7   Helen: parent governor and special needs assistant

conditioned by her long association with the school and by her extrovert personality. Helen believes that the role of governor is to contribute to the support of the school at every level in which governors have competence, and her main concern was the lack of time and training which prevented her fellow-governors from fully implementing their role under the 1988 Education Act.

> I never would have believed that there was so much to learn about our responsibilities. I have had time to find out things but I pity the new parent governor [an election was due to take place] though I shall certainly help her. There are courses, and handbooks, but working-class people like us aren't used to learning like some of the better educated governors. But I keep my end up!

As a special needs general assistant, largely untrained other than within the school, she showed a rapport with the small group of special needs children that experienced teachers might well envy:

> The best thing about the way this school is run is the attitude of the children to learning. Having had two children through the school I am much happier with the way things are now, especially for any children with learning difficulties.
>
> [And in her role as governor:] Wearing several hats, as it were, I feel I know far more about the way the school works and I am able to help parents to understand our aims and methods.

General

That almost all the teachers interviewed ranged from the relatively inexperienced to what might be termed the moderately experienced is unsurprising in view of the short time in which the headteacher had been introducing and implementing her plans for the development of an effective school. That the new deputy, after only four terms, was showing signs of being well on the way to being a renewing user – and thus a valued support to the headteacher – is encouraging both for her and for the headteacher. That she had at this stage relatively high concerns over management is understandable. She, too, will have felt the pressures of an unfamiliar role for which her previous experience had not prepared her and of the need for the rapid development of policies and practice if the school is to maintain its commitment to sound management and pupil learning.

The scattergram below (Figure 5.8) enables us to visualise staff concerns as a whole. There are clear indications in (1) and (2) that the rate of change that the headteacher, as school leader, considered vital if the school was to make rapid progress towards effectiveness was leading to high concern in, above all, the area of management. This is borne out by the interview transcripts, where comments about lack of time frequently appear. The high level of concern for consequence, on the other hand, shows a school staff committed to the achievement of the school's pupils. Surprisingly, perhaps, the teachers do not yet see themselves as a collegiate unit; however much they may be seeking to achieve in their own classrooms, there is no strong evidence of the collaboration one would expect to see, especially among the job-share teachers, though it is known that one of the two pairs meets

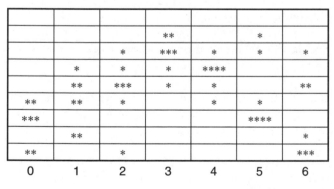

			**		*	
	*		***	*	*	*
		*	*	*	****	
	**	***	*	*		**
**	**	*		*	*	
***					****	
	**					*
**		*				***
0	**1**	**2**	**3**	**4**	**5**	**6**

Key:　0 Awareness　　1 Informational　2 Personal
　　　　3 Management　　4 Consequence　5 Collaboration
　　　　6 Refocusing

Figure 5.8　West Town Lane Infants School scattergram

weekly, out of school hours, to discuss pupil progress and plan the next week's work. In general, low concern for collaboration may well be a concomitant of high concern for time management.

The scattergram (Figure 5.8) supports the conjecture from the SoC interviews that staff were only now finding their feet in the much-changed circumstances of the school's aims and objectives. It is likely that now, over a year later, further interviews would take most, if not all, into the category of experienced users, and one or two into that of renewing users.

Summary

The summary for this and the subsequent case studies broadly follows the ten criteria for the effective school established by Mortimore (1993).

There is a strong, positive leadership emanating from the top, as is only to be expected in a school that has undergone, and is still undergoing, radical change. There is evidence of a growing collegiality as staff become more sure of themselves and as those who were in post under the previous headteacher adapt themselves to the new regime.

Aims and values are clearly stated, not least in the mission statement, to the formulation of which staff and governors contributed. The school development plan, in which the rolling programme of innovation and review is finely balanced, is structured to deliver these aims. The main focus is on teaching and learning, as can be seen from the rolling review of all subject curricula, but more particularly this focus is demonstrated through the ongoing informal discussions among staff. In this small school the interchange of pedagogical skills and methodology appears to take place without much prompting. Procedures for assessing pupil progress are well established; the keeping of individual records is time-consuming, but its importance is well understood by staff. The introduction of portfolios of representative student work as a means of setting standards in all subjects is a growing practice. Photographic records are an unusual feature of a school's record keeping, and are obviously a valuable adjunct.

There is a healthy atmosphere within the school among staff and pupils and a belief that their school is successful. In the classrooms there is considerable evidence of the pupils' work which is well displayed. The entrance is not only attractive but informative, so that parents are made aware, when they collect their children, of what is happening in the school. The foyer is also well laid-out, with photographs of all members of staff, both teaching and ancillary.

In an area of predominantly upper-working-class families, there are high expectations of their children's success in these early years: parental support is evident and most help their children, particularly through the use of the 'dialogue box' for reading progress in which both staff and parents make regular entries. Steps are being taken, for example a guide for parents on reading with their children, to promote greater awareness among parents of their role in their children's education. The attendance of parents at the 'work-alongs' is remarkably high. As mothers bring the children to school and collect them at the end of the day there is a notable atmosphere of relaxation and camaraderie.

Unusually for an infants school, pupils are involved in decision making within their classrooms over a wide range of issues, not least behaviour. Good work and good conduct are recognised by staff appreciation and by the headteacher as she visits classes. Commendation is passed to parents on an informal basis between the more formal occasions of staff–parent interview evenings.

The involvement of parents in activities that relate to the school and not solely to the learning of their own children is growing, as the work groups on cataloguing and maintaining books and equipment indicate.

6

KATES HILL SCHOOL

Introduction

Kates Hill is an inner-city primary school of 380 pupils with, in add-ition, a sixty-place nursery unit that provides 100 half-day places and, for a limited number of hardship cases, up to ten full-day places. Three out of four pupils are from non-white families, a small number from Afro-Caribbean or mixed-race families, but well over half the total school roll is of Asian origin, mostly from Pakistan immigrant families. The multi-ethnic composition of the school and community has profound implications for the way in which the school has addressed the issues of its role and function.

The nursery is staffed by a superintendent and four NNEB nursery nurses; the school, by the headteacher and sixteen assistant teachers, and the equivalent of eight ancillaries: general assistants, section 11 teachers, and learning-support teachers. The general quality of the staff is indicated by the fact that job turn-over is mainly through promotion, usually within the authority.

The present headteacher was appointed in 1986. The two members of staff who were in the school during the predecessor's incumbency summed up his management style thus:

- He made *ex cathedra* decisions about which only the deputy was informed before they were promulgated to the staff.
- He had little communication with other members of staff, encouraged no discussion, rarely sought opinions.
- The management structure was nominal, staff having no overt respon-sibility to or for each other. There were no assigned middle-management roles, and staff who received enhanced salaries for curriculum respon-sibility were in fact responsible only for the provision and organisation of the material resources for teaching.
- There was only the most formal relationship with parents, usually over matters of discipline, and no attempt to promote staff recognition of

the problems of those students who did not have English as their first language.

• Schemes of work were inflexible and staff were required to implement them rigidly. Content and methodology were never reviewed and consequently much of what was written down was out of date.

This last concern was the one that staff, in the discussions that the new headteacher held immediately after her appointment, were most anxious that the school should address. A rolling programme of reviews of schemes of work was immediately initiated.

Developments in organisation and management

The appointment of the new headteacher coincided with the allocation of some funds for building improvements. Money had previously been spent in carving up the purpose-built open-plan school into little boxes which served to isolate and exclude. She was convinced that the first stage of development must be a physical restructuring, to create areas of group responsibility in which communication would flow laterally and vertically. The boxes were opened up into year-group areas and the responsibility for their management given to a team of middle-managers. This innovation, which was both structural and organisational, provided the opportunity for the headteacher to initiate discussions on the nature and scope of these new responsibilities.

Staff meetings brainstormed curriculum development within the school in terms of content, resources, methodology and assessment. The school now had a mission statement which 'reflects the cultural diversity of the area it serves. It aims to serve the community by providing quality teaching and learning where the needs of all individuals are met.' The mission statement was translated into a statement of specific aims (see Table 6.1) which are revisited from time to time as part of the monitoring process to which reference is made later in this chapter.

The previous policy, that parents may not appear on school premises without appointment, became one of open access. While this was welcomed in principle by staff, in its early days it inevitably imposed stress on those teachers as yet ill-equipped to respond. Staff still saw their classrooms as their exclusive territory and felt vulnerable whenever visiting parents, children from other classes, or colleagues observed what was going on. Gradually there was recognition that parents kept in ignorance of what was happening in classrooms would fill the gaps in their knowledge with pure invention. Parent partnership evolved slowly, since the culture of the majority and their experience of the previous administration continued to be dominant.

To encourage the movement to openness, the administrative staff were relocated to assist parents and visitors as they enter, notices in ethnic

Table 6.1   Statement of aims: Kates Hill School

Statement of aims	
To ensure that each child	Reaches his/her academic potential
	Takes ownership of learning
	Is a responsible and reliable member of society
	Is valued and appreciates all cultures and traditions
	Develops self-esteem
And further to have	Parents in partnership
	The community reflected in the school
	The school reflected in the community
And for the staff to be	Reflective teachers

languages give helpful directions, and photographs of staff, teaching and ancillary, are sited prominently in the foyer. Regular newsletters in the community's main ethnic languages communicate to parents information about the school and invitations to events. A room is assigned to provide a comfortable, non-threatening setting for parent conferences.

What was achieved over the next three years was no more than the evolution from a rigidly hierarchical organisation to an open, community-oriented, school. Concurrently, however, the headteacher was building on the change process that had been initiated, taking the school into major new areas of pedagogy and staff involvement in decision making, including the adoption of a problem-solving strategy called GRASP® (Getting Results and Solving Problems).

The GRASP® innovation

The headteacher had been involved, in the period before she took up her new post, in a collaborative exploration with colleagues and teacher-training students in using problem-solving techniques within the classroom. As a consequence of this experience the chief adviser invited her to contribute to the LEA's application for funding from the Comino Foundation as a pilot site for the GRASP® project.

The problem-solving process is based on target setting and action planning:

• Select the purpose or objective and the success criteria.
• Generate different ways of achieving the purpose or objective; compare with the criteria and select the most promising.
• Put the chosen plan into operation; control the process.
• Review continually and check the results.

A two-day residential workshop in team building was run for management teams of the first cohort of schools engaged in GRASP® as part of the research documented in this book. One activity was the use of the Belbin questionnaire on team roles. Towards the end of the 1970s researchers in management performance in industry and commerce found that individual management skills alone were inadequate to ensure successful team working. The totality of team roles must be covered. A lack of members able and prepared to undertake certain roles, or an abundance of members with the same attributes in competition for the same role, unbalances the team and reduces its capabilities. Belbin (1981) undertook a long-term study of the performance of highly successful business management teams and came up with eight roles: company worker, chairperson, shaper, plant, teamworker, resource investigator, monitor–evaluator, completer–finisher. He evolved a self-perception inventory to enable team members to assess their strengths and weaknesses in each category. Not every team will have eight members, and some doubling-up may be necessary. Often the inventory does no more than state the obvious to the individual, though its findings, when shared by the team, may serve to emphasise to other team members that person's suitability for the role. There are times, however, when the outcomes of the inventory can radically change a team's perceptions of who ought to be doing what. That was so in the case of Kates Hill School.

Had the headteacher been asked to identify her role-type in advance of the inventory, she would have seen herself as the natural chairperson. In fact, though her score in the Belbin questionnaire was high for this role, all indications were that she was an outstanding shaper – defined by Belbin as one who 'continually attempts to influence the team's objectives, discussions and decisions'. Moreover, there was no other member of the team able to fill this role. Yet the then deputy headteacher had the attributes of chairmanship, and the team felt that this should be his role and that the headteacher's talents should be used where they would be of most value to the management of the school. Since the staff had already decided that their immediate use of GRASP® would be to develop collegiality underpinned by trust, good planning and effective delegation within staff teams, that decision would have been undermined if the headteacher had not accepted the corporate view. Fortunately, she recognised the contribution such a move would make to staff morale and team building.

Using the GRASP® decision-making process brought home to staff that collegiality is a term that describes a managerial style, and is not in itself a means of reaching a desired end. The result of using the process at all staff meetings was that staff became bonded by a clear understanding of the purpose and criteria of their endeavour, and less likely to take up factional or personal stances.

Thus far change within the school had been concerned mainly with the professional relationships and roles of the staff, both teaching and ancillary.

The advent of the National Curriculum now required the application of the GRASP® problem-solving approach to the task of coping with rapid curriculum development. One immediate consequence was the change from the current practice of curriculum development by curriculum leaders to that of curriculum teams and a significant reconsideration of roles and relationships.

The GRASP® process is more than a management tool. The national focus on curriculum development now became a major incentive to apply it also to the management of learning in the classroom. Three propositions form the basis of GRASP®:

1 People have a desire to be recognised and appreciated.
2 Everyone can be an achiever.
3 People can develop their talents and achieve recognition by undergoing a learning process.

In the classroom GRASP® translates to a four-pronged process. First, teachers share the purpose of learning and identify the criteria for success. A brain-storming session follows, aimed at generating ideas of how the learning can be achieved. The ideas are discussed and an action plan is formulated. Finally, the exercise is reviewed by pupils and the teacher to gauge its effectiveness.

GRASP® gives children an insight into and a say in what they learn. When children come into the school, [staff] assess their abilities and give them realistic goals. Achieving their aims greatly increases the children's self-esteem and spurs them on to better achievements.

(Williams 1992: 3)

GRASP® practices now permeated a wide range of activities. At the end of its introduction to the first cohort of schools, a full evaluation of the effectiveness of the innovation took place (Jones 1988). The responses of Kates Hill teachers cannot be separated from those of the other seven primary schools in the survey; but, of the thirty-nine primary-school respondents, thirty-seven were using GRASP® individually and thirty-four in collaboration with other teachers. The three most effective uses of GRASP® by these teachers were planning and preparation (thirty-four teachers), working with colleagues (thirty), and involving pupils in setting objectives (twenty).

Kates Hill used the findings of the report to consolidate and develop its own GRASP® practices. The school instituted as part of its in-service activities review sessions for existing staff and introductory sessions for new staff: 'All new staff have had initial training. A new coordinator took over responsibility for GRASP® and half-termly meetings have been held' (Development Review 1989–90).

High Scope

Kates Hill nursery staff have always accepted the need to work in close harmony with the main school, so that those children who move from pre-school into the school's Reception classes have a similar experience of responsibility for their own learning. The GRASP® methodology was eminently suited to decision making by the superintendent and her NNEB staff, but for the children in the nursery classes collaborative decision making was not considered appropriate. Yet something comparable to GRASP® was needed, and in the early 1990s the nursery investigated High Scope.

This programme has been used for pre-school children in the USA for over thirty years. In 1989 the British High Scope Institute was set up.

> High Scope is based on the premise that children should be encouraged, from a very early age, to make informed decisions, to be responsible for their own world, to plan and review their work. ... Children also need a regular daily routine ... [and] teachers, nursery nurses and parents who can help them to gain the skills they need, extending and broadening them all the time. This is done in the following ways:
> - organising the workspace so that it is logical and interesting
> - labelling apparatus clearly so that the children can be independent
> - carefully planned adult participation
> - a daily routine based on PLAN DO REVIEW.
>
> (Page 1990: 1)

The active learning concept has much in common with GRASP®, but there are significant differences reflecting the respective ages and stages of development of the children. The nursery team began by comparing their current practices with the High Scope curriculum and methodology and by introducing elements of the scheme as and when it seemed appropriate. In 1995 the nursery staff undertook a radical review of their practices, and introduced High Scope as an integral part of their way of working.

The Just School Project

One of the merits of the GRASP® process is that it enables a school to evaluate whether the introduction of a further innovation is consonant with previous developments. The school's clearly defined sense of purpose meant that there now existed the ability to innovate without destroying the infrastructure. The involvement of Kates Hill in the Just School Project is a case in point.

In 1989 Sir Maurice Shock, President of the Social Morality Council, convened a working party drawn from several LEAs with the remit to investigate

> the research evidence and practical issues involved in attempts deliberately to organise institutional life in such a way that pupils may learn moral concepts and become committed to them.
> (Social Morality Council 1989: 1)

The Council cited research on the effectiveness of good schools, Rutter *et al.* (1979) in particular, which suggested that, if schools become concerned with the moral dimension, they also enhance their effectiveness as learning institutions. The working party proposed three goals for learning about justice: knowledge and understanding, attitudes, and skills.

The headteacher perceptively realised that the skills required for the project were consonant with those of GRASP®. For the implementation of justice the Council concluded that pupils need to learn:

- social skills, expressing their views and listening to the views of others;
- the operation of arbitration and decision-making procedures;
- the collection and presentation of evidence;
- the organisational skills required for social action and that 'through practical experience they will learn that they can . . . develop the moral dispositions required for more autonomous action'. The decision to develop a moral education programme in Kates Hill was to lead to a rethinking, not of the school's management processes, since these were now well established to sustain change, but of the relationships among staff, pupils and parents.

Asian and Afro-Caribbean schoolchildren are often caught between two cultures. Normally hard-working, obedient, law-abiding, and respectful, some become influenced to adopt behaviours that are unacceptable in school and that confuse and distress their families. Despite the time and effort spent by Kates Hill staff on developing relations with the parents, petty thieving, playground bullying, misbehaviour in the school toilets and during the school assembly were on the increase. There was a growing tendency for parents to blame the school and the school to blame the home.

The potential of a moral education approach that drew on 'the social experience of life within the school and the community' (Rutter *et al.* 1979: 6) for improving behaviour, and consequently learning, led to the preparation of a position paper, discussed extensively by staff, and then to the development of an agreed school policy which became operational in 1992. Staff were aware that their present policies had taken them part of the way along the road, but not far enough. Children can contribute positively or negatively to the relationship between home and school. The open school policy was a major step forward, and the appointment of a Muslim woman able to speak with parents in their mother tongue had greatly enhanced communication. Mothers came regularly to activities in a mobile classroom installed alongside the nursery unit. However, it was noteworthy that most Asian mothers formed subgroups and took little part in discussions.

Now something of profound significance was being asked of all parents: to become involved in behaviour-modification contracts, in discussion and counselling sessions, in trusting the school and earning the trust of the school. They were also being invited to think beyond the behaviour of their own child/children and about the behaviour of the peer group. This required of the school's multicultural community a radical reappraisal of its own role. There was a growing recognition of the differences in behavioural norms both within the culture, as the ethnic group became assimilated, and across cultures. In a process of this kind the school cannot control outcomes; it can only act as a catalyst. Yet, in spite of such limitations, there was a developing awareness of changing attitudes in the community.

This was given effect through the home–school contract ('home–school partnership' is now the preferred term) which originated in a collaboration between the National Association of Head Teachers (NAHT) and the Royal Society of Arts (RSA). The vehicle for the introduction of the contract is an interview, sometimes a series of interviews, between parent, teacher and child. The aims of the partnership are:

- to encourage communication between home, school and child;
- to create an ethos of understanding and openness;
- to developing a shared commitment to common aims while encouraging individual responsibility;
- to have a vehicle which allows schools to fulfil obligations to parents by informing them of objectives, programmes of study and assessment procedures;
- to work together to develop each child to his or her full potential by having respect for each other, including the ability to negotiate outcomes.

The partnership creates a focus for discussion, preventing misunderstanding, and ensuring that all are involved and valued. Any feeling among parents of 'being sent for' no longer exists, certainly not among those whose children entered the school after the partnership was firmly established.

Quality control and BS 5750

When staff roles and responsibilities were reassessed to meet the demands of the National Curriculum Education Reform Act of 1988, Kates Hill decided that the headteacher and senior management team must not be exempted from a thorough reconsideration of their functions. Accordingly, after much discussion, a new and, for schools, highly original management structure was devised, consisting of boundary, resource, personnel and quality curriculum managers. Their responsibilities were defined as:

1 *Boundary manager* (headteacher):
   • to define and document the school's policies, the curriculum, resources and commitment to quality;
   • to deliver a quality service;
   • to contract with school governors for periodic review;
   • to identify staff training needs;
   • to meet the needs of the community.

2 *Resource manager* (deputy head):
   • to deploy finances in relation to staffing, premises and curriculum needs;
   • to manage resources and to lead the staff resources team.

3 *Special needs/Personnel manager*:
   • to coordinate the special needs provision throughout the school;
   • to be responsible for the welfare and deployment of staff;
   • to maintain training records.

4 *Quality manager*:
   • to monitor and control all areas of the curriculum;
   • to lead the quality team.

Kates Hill decided to define quality as 'meeting client requirements', the clients being parents, pupils and eventual employers. The school now took the decision that was to involve fourteen months of hard work, in particular for the headteacher and the quality controller, of translating a management structure into a management process. It was to become the first primary school to meet, with the help of a consultant, the stringent conditions of the British Standards Institution, BS 5750.

The key task was to compile the BSI 'Top Level Manual'. Many of its clauses did not at first seem applicable to schools. Yet this was to prove illusory: process control, for example, clearly related to the delivery of the curriculum, and the requirements for document control made the school aware of the inadequacy of its present procedures and impelled it to create an 'up-to-date library of all . . . documents referred to in school and in the procedures'.

For the first time the system of managing the school was precisely documented. All schools are now required by law to have a variety of documents: staff handbooks, guides for parents, and, increasingly, those that arise from the proliferation of DfEE circulars, and most of these will have come about by a process of accretion. The task of updating existing documentation is often subordinated to more immediate tasks. The British Standards' requirement is that these management procedures have a similar format and a standard exactitude. In schools 'who does what' is often not precise and 'what will be done if . . . ' is frequently left to individual initiatives. Boundary management concerns itself with major issues, while the classroom teacher is often faced with minor issues for which there is no clear guidance.

There will always be the need for off-the-cuff decisions at all levels of school management and no list of procedures set out in BS 5750 will ever be a satisfactory substitute for teacher initiative and corporate responsibility. Nevertheless, there is evidence from the annual BSI audit that since the school achieved the status of a BS 5750 registered 'firm' the quality of organisation and management has steadily improved the quality of learning.

The headteacher, at a conference organised by the Institute of Quality Assurance, assessed the way in which BS 5750 has contributed to the rubric established by Corbett (1990) that 'a social system's structure is its pattern of rules, roles and relationships. Restructuring represents a change in these social characteristics.' In her paper, the headteacher demonstrated that:

- The *rules* which represent the common understanding about what is and what ought to be are set down in the Top Level and Procedures Manual. These shared values have brought about a change in the climate and ethos of the school.
- The *roles* [include] the responsibilities of all teachers and ancillary staff and the accepted way these are carried out. BS 5750 has ensured that everyone knows who does what and how they do it.
- To achieve restructuring, *relationships* need to be achieved and new ones created. The process of achieving BS 5750 has enabled all staff to develop a more professional, organised approach to their work. This ensures [the status of] teachers as managers in all aspects of their work.
- The *result* is a more effective school.

(White 1993)

Stages of Concern interviews

Eight members of staff, based on a cross-section agreed by the author and the headteacher, were interviewed. There was, for domestic reasons, a gap of eighteen months between the first five and the last three interviews.

Geraldine: deputy manager for quality

Staff in any primary school, especially the more experienced and senior, have multiple responsibilities. Geraldine is no exception. She has fifteen years' teaching experience, seven in this school. She has therefore been heavily committed to the development of the whole range of innovations that constitute the school's drive towards restructuring. Her previous experience in industry as a personnel manager made her an ideal choice for the team of four who piloted the development of BS 5750 for the school. She took on the role of deputy manager for quality and internal auditor for BS 5750. The demands of this key post did not seem in any way to daunt her:

> Once we had completed the fourteen months of preparation the actual maintenance, though intensive, is clear-cut. We have thorough guidelines which make monitoring staff and student progress actually easier than before.

Her other key responsibility is for special needs. In a school with many children from families where English is not the home language the organisation of support is vital. She has initiated the 'breakthrough project', intensive language support for these pupils in an early morning session, during the lunch hour and after school. There is also a scheme for helping Asian mothers with basic English. The school–family partnership is thriving.

The CBAM profile for Geraldine (Figure 6.1) matches that of the 'model' renewing user, except in collaboration. This, she felt, was a consequence of

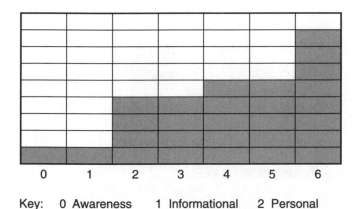

Key: 0 Awareness   1 Informational   2 Personal
      3 Management   4 Consequence   5 Collaboration
      6 Refocusing

Figure 6.1   Geraldine: deputy manager for quality with 15 years' teaching experience

lack of time to engage in all that she considered important. The high level of management concern endorses this.

Hilary: music teacher

Hilary has four years' teaching experience, all at Kates Hill. Her main responsibility is music, within the creative arts' curriculum area. She is also GRASP® coordinator, with responsibility for recording and testing. She is dynamic and hard-working as I became aware when in 1994 I was a guest at the school's annual performance that combined dance, music and drama and involved half the pupils of the school. Hilary has firm and constructive ideas on most aspects of the school restructuring policy, which she wholeheartedly supports.

As a teacher of a mixed-year class – Years 4–5 – with a wide range of ability, she is well aware of the need for all KS2 staff to have common standards of assessment.

Collaboration among staff, she felt, was high. When there was a disruptive child who could not be contained within the classroom, any member of staff who was in a position to do so would help by removing the offender.

Hilary's CBAM profile is complex (Figure 6.2). She expressed her concern over time management, but agrees that this arises because she willingly commits, possibly over-commits, herself to a whole range of time-consuming activities. Her constructive involvement in so many areas of school activity is clearly indicated by her high level in refocusing (6).

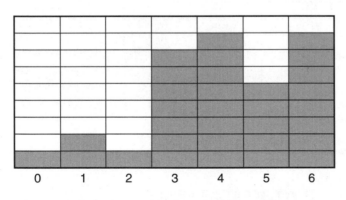

| 0 | 1 | 2 | 3 | 4 | 5 | 6 |

Key: 0 Awareness   1 Informational   2 Personal
       3 Management   4 Consequence   5 Collaboration
       6 Refocusing

Figure 6.2   Hilary: music teacher with 4 years' experience

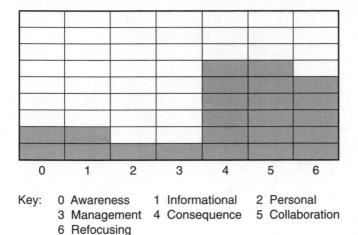

Key: 0 Awareness   1 Informational   2 Personal
       3 Management   4 Consequence   5 Collaboration
       6 Refocusing

Figure 6.3   Irene: parent governor and part-time teaching assistant

Irene: parent governor and part-time assistant

Irene is a parent governor, reaching the end of her service on the governing body since her children are all now beyond primary-school age. Her experience of the school extends beyond this role: she works part-time on the reading-recovery programme. She is well informed about all aspects of school policy. She is impressed by the school's documentation, though she is concerned that most governors do not find the time to study it as deeply as they should. She has, of course, been involved as a parent in the school–family partnership, and she has valued it for herself as well as for all parents. She finds a high degree of collaboration among staff, in which she is involved even though she is not a qualified teacher or a full-time member of staff.

Bearing in mind that she has only five hours a week of pupil-contact time it is not realistic to view the profile (Figure 6.3) in direct comparison with those of the full-time teaching or ancillary staff, but it is nevertheless illuminating.

Karen: nursery superintendent

Karen has a total of twenty-five years' experience, five of them in this school. Her main role is that of nursery superintendent, with a staff of four nursery nurses, one of whom is Asian and is specifically responsible for language development, and two half-time special needs assistants. There were also, at the time of the interview, two mature students under her supervision, one a mother of a child in the school, studying for the NVQ in Child Care.

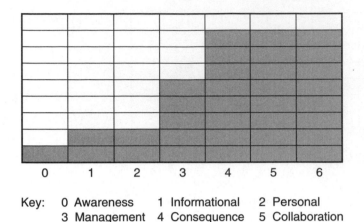

Key: 0 Awareness   1 Informational   2 Personal
      3 Management   4 Consequence   5 Collaboration
      6 Refocusing

Figure 6.4   Karen: nursery superintendent with 25 years' experience

She explained, with some wry amusement, that in addition to being in full charge of the nursery unit, she was responsible for monitoring and developing the mathematics curriculum for Key Stage 1 and was in charge of the foundation subjects.

Karen felt herself to be fully aware of the restructuring innovation as a whole, and to have minimal personal concerns (Figure 6.4). She appeared to carry her management responsibilities with ease, largely by involving all the nursery staff in decision making. She was kept well in touch with senior management discussions, though she did not attend team meetings unless she felt there was a matter of relevance to her work.

All work in a good nursery gives a prominent role to consequence, and she placed this, as was apparent in her views on management, as a very high concern. Her use of High Scope (see p. 85) is child-centred, although underpinned by precise educational aims.

Especially within the nursery, but on her own self-assessment also very much within the school as a whole, she rated collaboration highly, dismissing any idea that the nursery might be a 'separate domain'. She and her staff have consistently looked at possibilities for development and have explored in practical ways – the layout of the nursery area, for example, in relation to the children's learning programmes – major areas of refocusing. There is no doubt that her profile is that of a renewing user.

Laura: nursery nurse/teacher

With six years' experience in the nursery, Laura, a NNEB-trained nursery nurse, is clearly well integrated with the school as a whole. Her

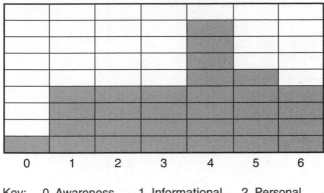

Key: 0 Awareness   1 Informational   2 Personal
      3 Management   4 Consequence   5 Collaboration
      6 Refocusing

Figure 6.5 Laura: nursery teacher with 6 years' experience

informational concern was high, but she appreciated that, with the nursery in a separate building, it was not always possible to keep herself up to date about, for example, information that appeared on the staff room notice board.

At a higher level, that of major school developments, she felt herself to be adequately informed, and interested in their application to the field in which she worked.

Her personal and management concerns support this (Figure 6.5); neither is of an unexpectedly high level, given the conditions of her professional involvement. What is particularly interesting, however, is her high concern for consequence (4). She sees the philosophy and planning of the work of a nursery nurse as directly relevant to the social and educational development of the children. Within the nursery there was a high level of team collaboration and a lack of assumption of status. Her high level of refocusing (6) was possibly a consequence of the extensive replanning in which the nursery team had just been engaged; yet she also showed herself to be aware of the need for a constant search for better ways of doing things.

Michael: coordinator of English[1]

Michael is in his third year of teaching and is coordinator of English. He completed his BEd at the age of 24, having travelled widely for several years prior to higher education, and is now working on his final dissertation for a Master's degree in linguistics. The urge to travel is still with him, possibly now combined with teaching English overseas.

[1] This interview and the two which follow were conducted four terms after the previous interviews.

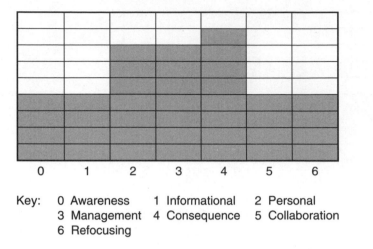

Key: 0 Awareness   1 Informational   2 Personal
       3 Management   4 Consequence   5 Collaboration
       6 Refocusing

Figure 6.6   Michael: coordinator for English with 3 years' experience

He finds paperwork irksome and regarded much of the preparation for the (then) forthcoming OFSTED inspection as unnecessary. 'External monitoring', he says, 'does not improve the quality of teaching and learning unless the motivation is there.' While he enjoys his work and responsibilities within the school, he feels strongly that there are too many outside pressures, and little freedom for the school to be adventurous in its teaching role (see Figure 6.6).

Naomi: senior coordinator for Year 5–6 group

Naomi, although a senior coordinator, spoke first with enthusiasm of her teaching role. She is team leader for the Year 5–6 group of ninety pupils. The mixed-age range, a consequence of the annual intake of forty-five, does not bother her. She and her three colleagues have devised strategies to minimise any adverse consequences.

The three team members plan their work together and, with KS2 assessments in mind, not only have routine cross-moderation exercises to do but often informally seek the opinion of a team colleague on the grade level for a particular piece of work. Of the key SAT subjects, maths and English take place in the morning and science, where she is able to utilise a fourth member of staff, in ability sets in the afternoon. One advantage that she sees is continuity in the teaching group from the previous year. She enthuses about the behaviour of the children and considers that they are setting a good example to the school, something that has not always been the case with the older group. One reason, she believes, lies in the increased responsibility which all Year 6 pupils are given: for example, a number of them help once a week to hear reading in the Reception class.

94

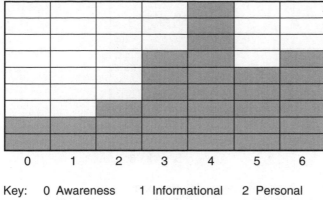

Key: 0 Awareness   1 Informational   2 Personal
      3 Management   4 Consequence   5 Collaboration
      6 Refocusing

Figure 6.7   Naomi: senior coordinator for Year 5–6 group

Her other management commitments, including quality control, are extensive, as she has taken on many of the responsibilities previous undertaken by the acting deputy headteacher, Penny (see below). She seemed to be taking them in her stride. Her extremely high level of consequence (4) indicates that it is her teaching role which is of greatest significance to her (Figure 6.7). Her lower collaboration (5) level she explains thus: 'I would place collaboration with my teaching team as high, but I have to balance this against what I have so far achieved with other members of staff in my other roles.'

Penny: acting deputy head

Penny was appointed acting deputy head early in the school year 1996–97 when it seemed most unlikely that the holder of that post would be returning from sick leave. She was at first daunted by the complexity of that role, since the senior master had left the school the previous Easter on promotion, and the headteacher had only recently returned from a sabbatical year as an associate OFSTED inspector. Her present role includes responsibility for the self-monitoring programme which she devised before assuming her present post.

She is now feeling far less stressed as she realises that, with good time management, she can perform the multiplicity of tasks for which she takes responsibility. She considers that one of the great steps forward since the return of the headteacher is the expansion of the senior management team to include all postholders. This, she believes, has done much to facilitate communication of policy decisions to all staff.

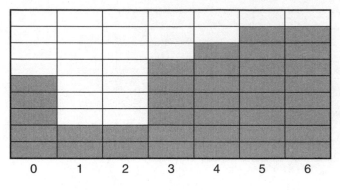

Key: 0 Awareness   1 Informational   2 Personal
       3 Management   4 Consequence   5 Collaboration
       6 Refocusing

Figure 6.8   Penny: deputy headteacher

Her 'self' concerns (0–2) are low (Figure 6.8): the higher level under awareness she ascribes to her present inability to see the school's change process as a whole. Management concerns (3) are understandably high as yet. The remaining concerns, especially refocusing (6), show her to be already a renewing teacher.

General

The scattergram (Figure 6.9) of this sample of the school staff demonstrates the extent to which the teachers have accustomed themselves to change and feel competent to innovate or to handle innovation. Four are very high on refocusing, yet four show a relatively high 'task' (management) concern, understandable in the light of the school's recent history. Consequence (4) and collaboration (5) are encouragingly high.

Summary

The leadership style of the headteacher has been consistent throughout her incumbency of the post. She has sought to develop corporate leadership, encouraging all staff, not only those in senior posts, to take on as much responsibility as possible within their assigned roles and also to contribute to the evolution of school policy. This policy has been an important factor in the success of a highly innovative school. The GRASP® project is one such innovation that the school has sustained long after the initial impetus for the scheme had ended in some LEA schools. The project has obviously been a major factor in providing a clear focus on teaching and learning, and High Scope in the nursery years is preparing children for the need to

0	1	2	3	4	5	6
				*		
				****	**	****
		*	**	*		
			**	*		*
*			*	*	****	
*	**	*	*		**	***
		**	*			
**	*****	**				
****	*	**	*			

| 0 | 1 | 2 | 3 | 4 | 5 | 6 |

Key: 0 Awareness   1 Informational   2 Personal
      3 Management   4 Consequence   5 Collaboration
      6 Refocusing

Figure 6.9   Kates Hill School scattergram

plan and evaluate their own learning achievements. The nature of the GRASP® project requires that pupils take responsibility for their own learning. Acceptance of this is a lengthy and continuous process. Displays of work around the school in all subjects contribute to setting standards. Staff demonstrate their acceptance of shared aims and values, and there is a general atmosphere among the staff of dedication to their work.

All visitors to the school feel welcomed by the reception area, where the secretary is immediately accessible, notices are in all the community's languages, and plants and a fish tank contribute to a soothing atmosphere. This is replicated around the school where the multi-racial nature of the neighbourhood is acknowledged, particularly in pictures and descriptions of the rich variety of religious festivals.

The staff are well aware that the relatively low expectation of pupils is a reflection of the conditions within the local community. Classes throughout the school are seen by visitors to be very much on task. Language difficulties, needing considerable support if they are to be overcome, have recently been exacerbated by cuts in Section 11 and other support staff.

The thorough maintenance of pupil progress records required by the National Curriculum, coupled with the stress placed by the school on collaboration with parents, is one of the school's major achievements.

The potential problems to which the multicultural environment might give rise have been recognised by the school and community and are increasingly being overcome by them working in tandem. The school's music and drama, participation in festivals and sporting activities, contributions to charity and involvement in the wider community are widely appreciated.

The school uses incentives rather than rewards. One of the most valued incentives is recognition, in the form of merit cards or simply through praise from teachers, of achievement or behaviour that enhances the image of the school. The school–home partnership plays an important role here.

7

RISCA PRIMARY SCHOOL

Introduction

The present headteacher was appointed to the headship of Risca Town Primary School in January 1992 to prepare for the amalgamation of that school and Danygraig Primary School into a school designed and built to meet the needs of education today. The move took place in May 1993 and the school now has a roll of 375 pupils with a further thirty-nine half-day pupils in the nursery. In addition to the headteacher there are fourteen teachers, six of whom were teachers at Danygraig or Risca Town, and four NNEB assistants, three specifically for special needs. As a matter of school and county policy a small Downs Syndrome specialised unit was integrated into the mainstream school. To meet both staff and parental anxiety, a programme of staff development was initiated. Fortunately, one of the staff transferring from a closing school possessed the Advanced Diploma in Special Needs and was appointed SEN coordinator; and in 1995 the school was able also to appoint a Key Stage 1 coordinator who holds the Certificate in Management of Special Educational Needs.

The school roll is distorted by the continuing existence of an infants school at the other end of the town. Consequently there is only one class in each of Years 1 and 2, then two thereafter. Of greater significance, perhaps, is that there has been insufficient coordination of curriculum policy between the two schools, which Mary Williams (1992) believes militates against effective curriculum integration in Year 3.

Risca was once a typical Welsh mining community, and might well have suffered the fate of many of south Wales's centres of population had it not been for the opening in the 1960s of a steelworks. To meet the needs of the incoming steel workers, British Steel built a number of housing estates in nearby towns. The estate lies on the hillside above the school. It is large enough to support its own infants and junior schools, and the local comprehensive school is also sited there.

When she took over the headship, the headteacher found no school development plan and no written curriculum policies. She did not attempt to remedy this deficiency before the staff of the new school were in post.

Her previous experience of headship in the West Midlands stood her in good stead. The LEA had been a leading authority in the introduction of appraisal, and she had been a member of the LEA primary tutor team. She had experience of planning and delivering staff and curriculum development and in the evolution of a school development plan. Although she deliberately set out to 'make haste slowly' the fact that she knew where she was going and how she intended to get there was to be important to the integration of the new school community.

Mission statement

The school's mission statement is a clear and concise statement of what the school intends:

- achieving excellence through learning, caring and sharing;
- children, parents, staff, governors and the whole community working together in a beautiful, richly resourced, school environment.

The school development plan makes it clear that this could be achieved only through a set of aims to which all the parties in the mission statement subscribe and which underpins all the school's work and efforts.

The school development plan

School development has first claim on the school's in-service provision. One of the five days annually allocated to INSET is devoted to the school development plan. The first such day took place in January 1993, to make provision for the financial year 1993–94. Since the first full academic year of Risca Primary School in its new buildings had been completed, the headteacher considered that an audit by the full staff, together with a representative of the governing body, should take place.

The first task was to undertake a strengths, weaknesses, opportunities, threats (SWOT) analysis that considered the six key areas of ethos, curriculum, staffing, management and organisation, the school community, resources. The analysis identified the greatest strengths in the areas of staffing, management and community. Management, for example, demonstrated the rapidity with which the school had developed a coherent policy, acceptable to staff. Curriculum and staffing were the areas of greatest concern (Table 7.1). The greatest threat was, not surprisingly, in the area of resources.

As a matter of urgency a scheme had been drawn up to create – where possible by the end of the academic year – documents covering each of the priority areas that were to constitute the school development plan. Each curriculum coordinator met with the INSET coordinator to plan an allocation of from one to five meetings and to decide the membership of the

Table 7.1   Strengths and weaknesses

Management strengths	Collegiate management
	Effective communication
	Matching budget priorities and the development plan
	Clear management links
	Long-term planning
	Clear targets set
Staffing weaknesses	The effect on staff morale of class size
	Need for additional male staffing
	Lack of some pockets of expertise

task group for that subject. The school management team, which consists of the headteacher, the deputy headteacher, the KS1 and KS2 coordinators and the INSET coordinator, was responsible for the drafting of the non-curricular policies: assessment, behavioural problems, job descriptions, for example. Each policy document is contained in a well-produced brochure.

The idea of the annual audit gave rise to a series of priority action plans. That for special educational needs is characteristic of the organisation that supports sound corporate management procedures. The one-page document names the convenor and the action group – in this case the special educational needs department (see Table 7.2). It also specifies the personnel, whether within the school or in the LEA, who can be called upon for guidance and expertise, and the time-scale for the production and publication of the policy document. The need to comply with the newly issued Code of Practice was instrumental in establishing an early completion date.

Table 7.2   Priority action plan: special needs

To review assessment procedures and the identification of models currently used to determine the children with special needs in the light of the Code of Practice

To identify organisational and managerial strategies for the effective teaching of these children

To develop links with the parents of these children

To institute regular review meetings between the class teacher and the parents to discuss progress

To hold regular year group meetings to determine the needs and progress of special needs children in that year

To organise individual files covering the total remediation activities of special needs children

To present the whole school policy on special needs to the staff and governors

The seven-point policy statement is a model of a feasible but thorough development strategy.

The curriculum

The school development plan is the medium for the evolution and evaluation of the curriculum and the facilities which support the curriculum. The curriculum area which deserves separate mention is the introduction of Welsh as the eleventh subject within the National Curriculum.

From the school year 1996–97 the teaching of Welsh had become compulsory throughout primary and secondary schools in Wales. In much of the Principality this poses no problem; in most north- and west-Wales counties and districts Welsh is the first language, and English a minority language. There are numerous schools in these areas of Wales in which the whole curriculum is studied through the medium of Welsh, and in those where English is the medium of instruction the study of the language, culture and literature of Wales is part of the national heritage.

The problems lie in the counties and districts bordering England, and Gwent is one such. It has therefore been necessary for Risca's teachers to have periods of secondment to learn the language and study textbooks and the teaching methodology. One teacher, now the curriculum coordinator for Welsh in addition to other responsibilities, undertook a one-term course of study. Others have had two-week secondments. Schools have received no additional financial resources for the in-service training or the books and equipment needed to equip the school to teach the subject to an effective standard. It is no wonder that the staff evaluated Welsh as an area of weakness in the SWOT analysis.

The second area of concern was the library provision. In the plans of the school the library can be seen to be ideally placed for access from the eight junior classrooms. It overlooks a delightful courtyard so that the quiet atmosphere is enhanced, and there is ample shelf space for books. The problem is that there are too few books. Those from the two schools that amalgamated to form Risca Primary School were not in a condition worthy of the new building. With over 300 junior children there should be at least 1,500 books. It is difficult for staff to encourage pupils to research and to read widely when the facilities are in short supply.

In contrast, the initial stocking of the school for information technology has been considerable. The funding came mainly from the LEA capital costs' budget for the new building.

Investors in People (IIP)

In 1995 the headteacher decided to apply for recognition under the Investors in People scheme:

I felt the need for some external recognition of the school's growing worth that would be of significance to the governing body and parents and would also recognise the hard work put in by teaching and ancillary staff. I also saw this as an opportunity for an external assessment of my management of the school.

In February the assessor interviewed staff, governors, ancillaries and pupils, and studied the school management documentation and future plans. There were only minor criticisms, easily remedied, and six months later the IIP plaque was presented. The certification requires a triennial review; this, the headteacher believes, is a form of continuing appraisal of her work and of the school as a whole.

The *Times Educational Supplement* Awards

In March 1996 The *Times Educational Supplement* announced that Risca Primary School had been selected, out of 700 schools that entered, for a TES Annual Report Award made to school governing bodies producing the clearest and most informative annual reports to parents.

In May 1996 the school was the recipient of another award, the TES School Prospectus Award, in association with Rank Xerox. The three prize winners, one in each category of primary, secondary and special school, received a photocopier.

The headteacher was in no doubt about her response to these questions: 'Achieving excellence is what we are working towards in everything we do and that includes the school prospectus.' Furthermore, the prospectus demonstrates the school's outward-looking philosophy.

Home–community links

The aims of the school priority action plan include:

* to extend home–school links within the school and classroom;
* to [make visible] within the community pupils' work, celebrations and the general life of the school.

With the new school year of 1995–96, there was a revival of PTA activity that was sedulously cultivated by the staff.

The 1995 Christmas play proved to be an important catalyst. In the headteacher's words:

The parents were buzzing! They had no expectation of the high quality of the performance. Parents are now coming in far more frequently on a casual basis, and there are early signs of a regular commitment from a few parents to helping in the classroom.

103

There are now termly class assemblies to which parents are invited, and they stay on for coffee and talk. Each September the year group comes to a 'Meet the Teacher' evening session and in the spring and summer terms there are one-to-one interviews on each child's progress. The staff handbook is very precise on the purpose of the review interview (see Table 7.3).

The school has an excellent hall, with a fully equipped stage and auditorium, the latter doubling as a mini-sports hall. The community is being encouraged to use these facilities, and their use will doubtless grow as more community groups in the neighbourhood of the school become aware of what is on offer. The school is fortunate in having a caretaker who understands the school's purpose in promoting community use. Decisions on lettings' policy are made jointly by the headteacher, the caretaker and the governors.

Stages of Concern interviews

Five members of the teaching staff and one NNEB assistant were interviewed individually in sessions lasting from thirty to forty-five minutes. All were very open, keen to explain their roles and full of admiration for their headteacher, who, they believed, was creating an excellent school of which they were proud to be a part.

Barry: Year 6 coordinator

Barry joined the school staff in September 1992 and has therefore seen the move to the new buildings and the totality of developments since. He is the Year 6 coordinator, and his special area of curriculum responsibility is information technology. He sees Conley's central variables as inseparable, a view which showed a recognition of the basic principles of restructuring.

> The curriculum is clearly the core driving force in school improvement, and the quality of teaching is contingent on the implementation of the curriculum policy. The curriculum

Table 7.3 Parent–child–teacher reviews

It must be a positive experience for the child, adult and teacher
It must be informal and non-threatening. If the adults find it valuable, word will spread
The children must . . . encourage their parents to come into school
If the parent does not come, then the child must still have a chat with the teacher

documents are, however, only as good as they prove to be, and we must therefore look at learner outcomes to ensure that our policies are effective. This implies careful monitoring and routine assessment.

Barry believes that the children are not yet working to their full potential: there was no sense of urgency or pride. This he thought was a consequence of the low expectations in the schools from which they had come when their present school opened, and which was likely to be less true of younger pupils than those in his Year 6 class, since they had spent their junior school years uninfluenced by previous experience in either Danygraig or Risca Town Primary School. He was also concerned that on the one-to-one parents' evening, while the turnout was high at twenty-seven out of the class of thirty-two, the parents who did not keep their appointments were those of the educationally weaker children.

He saw the school as beginning to integrate with the community. With little or no history of parent or community access to the previous primary schools, it was taking time to effect change. He appreciated that the development of curriculum policy was the first priority, but welcomed the increasing encouragement by the headteacher, governors and staff to the wider use of the school facilities.

His SoC profile is (Figure 7.1) that of a young teacher who has found his feet in the school and the profession. He is, in the language of the Concerns-based Adoption Model, on the way to becoming an 'experienced teacher', one clearly capable of developing.

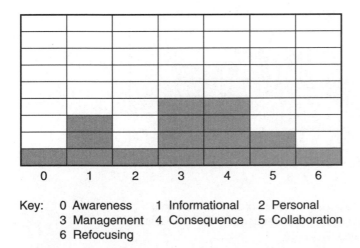

Key: 0 Awareness   1 Informational   2 Personal
      3 Management   4 Consequence   5 Collaboration
      6 Refocusing

Figure 7.1   Barry: Year 6 coordinator with 4 years' experience

Odette: KS1 coordinator

Odette was the most recently appointed member of staff, having come in January 1995 to the post of Key Stage 1 coordinator and teacher of Year 2. Her previous experience gave a valuable 'outsider's' view of Risca School. In common with all members of staff interviewed, she saw the curriculum policies as essential to the school's effectiveness. The policies were well structured and focused, but their delivery depended not only on the skills of the class teachers but also on the support given by the curriculum coordinators. Review of the policies needed to be ongoing, but full evaluation needed to be undertaken when there was better evidence of their success and shortcomings.

She felt that the 'hidden curriculum' was, in this school, of crucial importance and had herself promoted personal and social education in her class. The community policeman was a regular visitor to talk to the children in her class.

> Learner outcomes need to be monitored regularly. It is as important for pupils at the beginning of their school experience as for those higher up in the school to be aware of the progress they are making and any shortcomings in their work. While national standards are considered to be of importance by government, a school works to give added value to the pupils of its neighbourhood.

Odette also showed herself to be strongly committed to home–school relations, well beyond the formal occasions that the school organised:

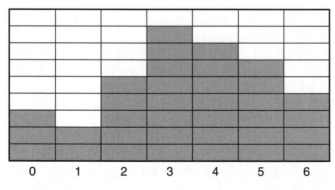

Key: 0 Awareness   1 Informational   2 Personal
      3 Management   4 Consequence   5 Collaboration
      6 Refocusing

Figure 7.2   Odette: KSI coordinator

This is a working-class district in which parental involvement in the school is not a tradition. I believe in being around to see any parents of the children in my class who come to discuss any matter that is worrying them. If it cannot be dealt with there and then, I make an appointment at the earliest convenient time.

Her profile (Figure 7.2) shows fairly high personal concerns, not atypical of a relatively new member of staff. Her management concerns were high as were her concerns for consequence: she currently views pupil progress as the key to the success of her role, and collaboration with staff as the way to achieve it in the areas of her responsibility as KS1 coordinator, a role she takes very seriously. She is likely to be of value to the school as it develops its curriculum policies over the next few years.

Paula: KS2 coordinator

Paula is the most experienced teacher in the school, having taught in the locality for nineteen years. She was a teacher in Danygraig Primary School before the new school was built on its site and the amalgamation with Risca Town Primary School took place. She presents herself as a teacher full of confidence, delighted to be in a school with 'a headteacher who knows what she is doing and intends to make this a first-rate school'. Her post is that of KS2 coordinator and she teaches one of the two Year 6 classes. At the time of the interview she had just been appointed acting deputy head-teacher, and she was later to be confirmed in that post by the governors when the opportunity arose.

She was insistent that the central variables were interdependent:

The curriculum determines the schemes of work. These are subject to assessment and evaluation, but we must be careful to guard against too rapid change, since this leads to staff insecurity. The staff as a whole are willing to declare any areas of weakness which they feel; and the advantage of working in pairs in Years 3–6 is inestimable since we can share the planning load and collaborate in all sorts of ways. Increasingly staff are addressing the strategies of teaching, without which good pupil performance is unlikely to happen.

The fact that Paula had lived most of her life within the town made her a great asset in school–community relations. She was able to attract ministers of religion to visit the school, and not solely to take assemblies. The town's librarian welcomed pupils who needed to research some aspect of the curriculum and also came into the classroom to talk about the facilities on offer. At the time of the VE-Day commemorations she had brought into the school parents and others who had experiences of those days to relate:

> One of them was actually an evacuee who had stayed on in Risca after the war and had married a local resident. This, and other experiences told at first hand, brought home to the children in a way that talks by staff could not the changes that war had brought about in our community.

She is prominent in the Parent–Teachers' Association, has promoted school links with local industry, and is looking forward to the even greater use of the school's facilities by community choirs and other groups. Not surprisingly, she finds parents very supportive of the school, though she acknowledges that they seem to be satisfied with standards of pupil achievement which are lower than they ought to be:

> Their expectations are too low. Our children are over-protected, not least the able ones. Whenever work gets difficult, mothers say: 'I don't want him/her to do that. All I want is that he/she is happy at school.' We try to reinforce success by honouring achievement in small stages. I am hoping we can introduce open evenings soon so that they can actually see what their children are supposed to be learning. So much of the curriculum is alien to their own experience.

Paula's profile (Figure 7.3) is high in the areas of consequence and collaboration, indicating a clear concern for pupil and staff progress. While

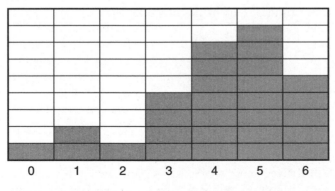

Key: 0 Awareness   1 Informational   2 Personal
       3 Management   4 Consequence   5 Collaboration
       6 Refocusing

Figure 7.3   Paula: KS2 coordinator with 19 years' experience

refocusing is not yet at the level that would lead to a description of her as a renewing user, she is undoubtedly interested in ways of improving what the school offers to the pupils, parents and community.

Rose: coordinator for SEN

Rose is the coordinator for special educational needs and was a member of staff of one of the schools amalgamated to form Risca Primary School. She sees her role within the promotion of the curriculum policies as mainly one of developing cooperation with staff and coordinating their approach to 'statemented' pupils and others in need of special attention. Curriculum differentiation is for her the key to the learning processes of these children.

With her team of three special educational needs NNEB assistants – two of them part-time – she visits classes to work with the teachers offering both observation and direct support. Additionally, each class has a daily half-hour reading session which the team supports as often as time allows. The policy of graded group reading is not appropriate to some special educational needs pupils, particularly the six statemented at Key Stage 5. For them, individual reading learning guided by a member of the team is vital.

For her, assessment and evaluation of the children's progress as well as of the action plans is a vital part of her role. Not surprisingly, she seeks to develop strong links with the parents of these children. She finds that, in general, parents are willing to help, but are unaware of what they should be doing. This is clearly a major obstacle to their learning at times.

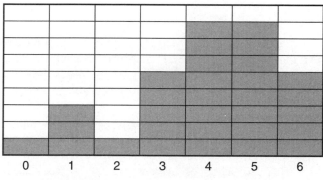

```
0    1    2    3    4    5    6
```

Key: 0 Awareness   1 Informational   2 Personal
       3 Management   4 Consequence   5 Collaboration
       6 Refocusing

Figure 7.4   Rose: coordinator for SEN

With the introduction of the Code of Practice, the amount of documentation required has increased considerably. Rose believes that schools can do this effectively only when the staff are willing, as they are in this school, to work cooperatively.

Rose has very much welcomed the introduction of regular staff appraisal by the headteacher: 'It is easy to feel isolated in a role like mine, and I value the opportunity for a thorough mutual investigation of what I am doing and what I plan to do.' Her profile (Figure 7.4) is that of an experienced teacher. She has few concerns at the first three stages. Her management concern reflects the complex nature of her role, and consequences for pupils and collaboration with staff are high.

Clive: INSET coordinator

Clive is the school's INSET coordinator and, as such, an important member of staff in a school with rapidly developing curriculum and management policies. He is also coordinator for the personal and social education curriculum and is one of the two Year 4 teachers.

For him, as with all staff, curriculum development has been the key central variable.

> When I joined the staff in September 1992 there was no curriculum policy. As we prepared for the amalgamation of the two schools the headteacher began to engage us in what I now realise was a massive task, to have curriculum and management policies in every field of the school's activities within three years. This was achieved for 95 per cent of the intended policies and the two outstanding policies, for science and information technology, were completed by March 1996.

The realisation that in this school policy writing is not just a paper exercise led him to realise that the role of INSET coordinator involved more than finding suitable courses for staff. Prioritising school needs brought him into a close working relationship with the headteacher, and he believes he has learnt much from this.

Undoubtedly influenced by the headteacher's own educational philosophy, he understands the symbiotic relationship between curriculum and learner outcomes. He sees a key task for all staff to be the raising of standards. He is reasonably optimistic that the school is overcoming the inertia that it encountered in its inheritance from the two previous primary schools. He holds the view, shared by most staff, that many children have more ability than they think – and their parents believe – they have: both need encouragement. The parental attitude of 'so long as they are happy . . . ', remarked on by Paula, needs to be extended to '. . . and hardworking and achieving'.

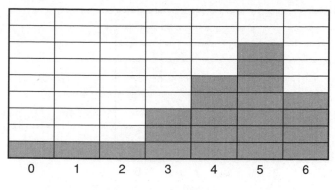

Key: 0 Awareness   1 Informational   2 Personal
        3 Management   4 Consequence   5 Collaboration
        6 Refocusing

Figure 7.5   Clive: INSET coordinator

He sees a need for the school to win the active collaboration of parents. This means sessions for parents so that they are familiar with changes in the curriculum and methodology that have taken place since they were at school.

He was rather dubious about the view held by some staff of the role of assessment and evaluation.

He sees as one aspect of his INSET role the establishment of good professional relationships with mutual respect and a willingness to negotiate over areas of disagreement. He values the non-contact time allowance for coordinators, since this promotes the opportunity for collaboration and negotiation (see Figure 7.5).

Sue: SEN assistant

Sue is an NNEB-trained special educational needs assistant. She came to Risca School in September 1994 to work particularly with a cerebral palsy child with whom she had already been working in a special unit. Her approach with all such pupils is one of stimulating them to achieve. Using a computer, she has trained this child in phonics so that she has some reading skills, but, most importantly, she has taught her that she is not a 'write-off'.

She finds working in the school an exhilarating experience and is devoted to the headteacher: 'You can talk to her at any time. You just knock on her door, ask "are you busy?" and she will see you straight away if she is free, or else make an appointment for you.'

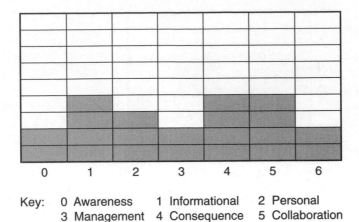

Key: 0 Awareness   1 Informational   2 Personal
       3 Management   4 Consequence   5 Collaboration
       6 Refocusing

Figure 7.6   Sue: NNEB-trained SEN assistant

She explained that she was a school failure, rubbished by her English teacher in particular as 'thick', because she was unable to spell. With her present headteacher's encouragement she has completed level 3 of the NVQ in Child Care and intends to proceed to level 4 and 'perhaps even level 5 eventually, who knows?' Her own educational experience took her a long time to live down, but has undoubtedly given her insights into learning difficulties.

She showed a mature understanding of the interdependence of the central variables and illustrated it by her own work with less able children in one of the years which was concerned with their own environment: Risca has a rich and varied history and she helped with canal studies, past and present. Her enthusiasm is infectious and her work is appreciated by the staff in general. Her SoC profile (Figure 7.6) is very much what would be expected of a good NNEB assistant.

General

The scattergram (Figure 7.7) indicates a staff, most of whom are experienced teachers, that has rapidly adapted to a period of intensive change. None have serious concerns in the 'self' elements (0–2). Management (3) is for one member of staff a concern of some importance, understandably in that she is a recently appointed member of staff and to a post of considerable responsibility. Consequence (4) is high, collaboration (5) is uneven, but evidence from the interviews suggests that this is a growth point. Refocusing (6) is not as yet a major concern of staff.

0	1	2	3	4	5	6
			*	*	**	
				**	*	
					*	
		*	*	*		**
	*		**	**	*	**
*	**	*	*			
*	**		*		*	*
****	*	****				*

Key: 0 Awareness   1 Informational   2 Personal
      3 Management 4 Consequence   5 Collaboration
      6 Refocusing

Figure 7.7   Risca Primary School scattergram

Summary

There is no doubt that Risca Primary School needed an effective leader, and the strength of the present headteacher lies in her clear perspective on the school's developmental needs allied to the ability to share the ownership of the way they will be met with the whole staff.

Both in interview and in their interpersonal relations, staff displayed a remarkably high corporate adherence to shared aims and values. The quality of the building design, with the pairing of classrooms and the general openness of work areas, is beginning to contribute to an increasing level of collaboration among staff. The policy documents initiated by the senior management team and developed by staff are now providing the necessary focus on teaching and learning. All staff interviewed were firm in their view that these were integral to the success of the school. Assessment procedures were at an early stage of development. The staff are as yet somewhat inhibited by what they regard as the LEA processes for assessment ('ticking boxes'), and the school is working to develop its own procedures.

Work by pupils was prominently displayed throughout the school. Displays of learning materials gleaned from the community linked the school with its environment. Nevertheless, pupil expectations were not high. The main difficulty to be overcome was actually the low expectation of many parents, typified by the attitude that staff encounter of 'so long as she/he is happy . . . '. That pupils should achieve their potential is certainly an aim of the school, but not one that will be realised in the short term. However, there was some evidence in visits to classrooms that pupils are beginning to take some responsibility for their own learning. This was more evident in Years 4 and below; Years 5 and 6 still bear the marks of the very formal teaching in their previous schools which did little to encourage pupil initiative.

There was no evidence of the school having adopted, or wishing to adopt, a rewards policy, but there were incentives, most obviously in the display of creative writing and art work in the headteacher's office and around the school.

Before the new school opened, there had been little encouragement of parental involvement. This was changing rapidly, with, for example, parents coming to a morning assembly and staying for coffee and discussion. Staff were united in linking activities such as this with higher pupil achievement and in believing that the school's open-door policy was beginning to make an impact on the parent body.

The school has a stated policy to develop extra-curricular activities. The 1995 Christmas play was rightly regarded by the headteacher as a catalyst, and further such activities feature prominently in the school's developmental aims.

8

PEERS SCHOOL

Introduction

Peers School was formed in 1968 when grammar and secondary modern neighbouring schools on the same site were merged under the city's programme for comprehensive education. It is a coeducational upper school (Years 9–13) with over 600 pupils. Those who enter at the normal age of transfer come from any of the middle schools in the city; others join the school in Year 11 for one to three years in the sixth form. The school takes its name in tribute to its first chair of governors, who had been chair of the county education committee and was renowned for his first-hand knowledge of and interest in the school.

The school lies within a council estate and serves that community in a number of ways. Many of the school's facilities, not least the sports and arts centre, are widely used in the evenings, at weekends and in school holidays. There is a programme of Saturday morning activities for children aged 5–13, which is not only a valuable community service but helps to facilitate the integration of those who reach the age of admission. There is a community education centre which offers a wide range of adult education classes to examination level, as well as providing social and recreational activities. The campus also houses the community library, a day nursery, a health and fitness centre, and Commercial Services, a business with fifty employees.

In addition to the normal curriculum, the school operates 'twilight courses' through which pupils can access additional GCSE examination subjects. There is also 'education plus' which offers a range of subjects including first aid, media studies, desk-top publishing, information technology, film animation, electronics–robotics and understanding art. By completing the course in any two of these, pupils qualify for a certificate.

More so than most schools in the county, Peers has pupils who find it difficult to work at home. For them the school has, with financial support from local industry, the Hamilton Trust and the Prince's Trust, equipped a room with computers, books and other resources and, most importantly,

115

has appointed a coordinator to support students with their work at the end of the school day. There are plans to open the centre at weekends and during school holidays.

Numbers in the sixth form have risen dramatically, from 15 per cent of the related age group in 1988 to 34 per cent in 1992 and 56 per cent in September 1995. This is a consequence in part of the encouragement given to students, and in part of the wide choice of A level and vocational courses. The recent introduction of GNVQ courses makes it likely that the percentage of pupils staying on into the sixth form will increase still further.

In 1995 Peers, having previously achieved a Technology in Schools Initiative award, was granted 'technology college' status by the DfEE. The funding for this, backed up by sponsorship from the business community, is enabling the school to upgrade its information technology provision to a high level, with new computers in each classroom, graphic calculators for mathematics, data-logging equipment for science and access to CD information and internet. The community library will be upgraded into a neighbourhood computerised information and literacy centre, with access to CD and the internet for the community as well as the school.

The school's strong links with industry have been recognised by the Education–Industry Partnership Award. It has twice, the maximum permitted, won the Schools Curriculum Award. It is a member of the Oxford partnership of Business in the Community.

Staffing and management structures

There are thirty-eight teaching staff and thirty support staff. Management is currently through a senior management team of six: the headteacher, the two deputy headteachers, the head of the sixth form, the examinations officer and the bursar. There are six curriculum areas: creative arts, English, mathematics, science, technology and learning support, each headed by a coordinator. Other subjects, such as modern languages and PE, come within what is called the 'community area' which also includes one of the two deputy headteachers, the examinations officer and the sixth-form coordinator.

The tutor groups play an important role in the school. Most students remain with the same tutor for three years. In Year 9 half the curriculum is taught in tutor groups, the other half in broad ability bands based on information from the feeder middle schools. The tutor is the first line of communication for parents. Each tutor group is represented on the school council. The school's publications in leaflet form cover such matters as rights and responsibilities, a policy about bullying and one on homework. These clearly delineate the boundaries of behaviour and the expectations of standards of work from students, and, with sex education, underpin the tutor's role in personal and social education.

116

These management structures were introduced by the headteacher when he was appointed in 1988. His predecessor had radically restructured the school organisation. He reorganised twenty departments, which were undoubtedly fragmenting the control of curricular policy, into six departments, but, as those who were on the staff at that time have indicated in interview, without carrying the staff as a whole with him.

The new headteacher appointment in 1988 coincided with the Education Reform Act which introduced extensive government control and direction. The school's annual budget, when allocated by the LEA, had previously been loaded in its favour in recognition of its social disadvantage. The loss of staff over the next few years was considerable. Nevertheless, local financial management was to become less a cross to be borne than an opportunity to involve staff in budgetary decision making and thus encourage team building and a concern for whole-school development rather than sectarian advantage. The new powers of the governing body, as will be seen in the next section, were beneficial to the school, largely because of the quality of its membership, but also because of the way the headteacher kept governors informed about and involved in the school's progress. The return to homogeneous curriculum teams has made it possible to absorb the demands for change imposed by the National Curriculum, not without stress, but certainly without significant loss of teacher morale.

Where there are no external time constraints on decision making, the headteacher is prepared to allow as much time as it takes to ensure that there is effective team work and, eventually, full agreement and support. The evolution of statements on behaviour, eventually published as leaflets that all new parents and their children receive, well illustrates this. It was necessary to change ingrained attitudes such as 'What do you expect from kids living on an estate like this? Having a policy on bullying will not stop it. Parents just do not care.'

The process was lengthy but effective, and illustrates both the headteacher's notion of decision making and his vision:

> If we say we want [young people] to be independent, autonomous, decision-making young adults, but tell them they must do exactly as we say, then they know we don't mean it. . . . I began a discussion with the Senior Management Team about what we, at Peers, ought to be able to expect from each other, whoever we are, in order to get on with our jobs at the school. From this we drafted a document which, in those days, we called a Code of Conduct and we put it to staff.
>
> (Anderson 1997)

Staff and student discussions were held and suggestions were used in further drafts of the policy, which was finally ratified by governors.

117

The results are evident in the mature behaviour of students around the school, the good interpersonal relationships between staff and students, and by the fact that visitors, and there are many, are free to go wherever they wish in the school.

The headteacher saw his key role as that of 'articulating the vision':

> My vision of leadership . . . is being responsible for creating the climate in which young people and adults can do their best. . . . My view of headship is of somebody who tries to articulate a set of principles, persuades people of those principles, and then puts them into practice.
>
> (Anderson 1997)

In his office, alongside pupils' art work and mementoes of school visits and visitors, is a salutary reminder that 'obstacles are what you see when you have lost your vision'.

The key management tasks of the school are currently to raise the status of the school in the eyes of parents and the wider community by improved examination results and by the school's becoming a model community in which good behaviour is the norm.

Assessment

The school sets great store by the six elements of its ongoing assessment procedure. The first, reports to parents, is common to most schools. These are annual and contain internal examination marks, Key Stage 3 results for Year 9 and predicted external examination grades for Year 11. They are collected by parents at parents' evenings, when discussion with tutors about progress takes place. Interview time is necessarily limited and appointments may be made for further tutor interviews. Additionally, parents are free to make appointments with tutors at any mutually convenient time, if they have concerns.

There is a clear marking policy, the format of which is the responsibility of each department, since a school-wide format is clearly impracticable. Allied with this are checkpoints, designed to monitor student progress, particularly work in class, homework and attendance. If there are difficulties remedial action is taken.

Reviews take place within each subject area at an appropriate time in the course, to enable students to reflect with their subject teacher on their progress and plan future improvements where necessary. Records of achievement, once heralded as no less important than examination results but now in most schools fallen into disuse, are given to all students on leaving school. The record is continuous and is designed to cover not only the statutory curriculum, but also social and extended learning achievements which would not be recorded elsewhere. Part of the certificate is a personal record written periodically by students under the guidance of tutors.

Above and beyond the assessments made by the students themselves, their subject teachers and their tutors, members of the senior management team engage in monitoring of learning: they interview each student at least twice a year to look at samples of work and homework diaries, and to discuss future aims and aspirations. This may seem excessively onerous for those in the top echelon of management, but the school is certain that the effect on staff, students and parents of this direct interest in pupil progress is considerable.

Outreach

The school produces a termly newspaper of high quality, both technically and in its contributions. In it, the school publicises its achievements – academic, extra-curricular and sporting – profiles new staff, gives students an opportunity to contribute and provides a diary of events.

One of the school's most remarkable activities is in its Tanzania link. This began in 1984 when the school linked with Katumba II in southern Tanzania. Since then there have been regular visits in each direction; in 1995 a group of students spent a month working alongside the Katumba students, living for two days in a rural community and spending a weekend with a Tanzanian family.

The 1996 spring term edition of the 'Peers Paper' typically reported on a number of outreach initiatives:

- A team from the school's Diploma Business Group took part in the Young Enterprise Trade Fair in January.
- The Passport Scheme, intended to provide an introduction to university life, has been introduced for Year 12 and 13 pupils in partnership with a local university.
- A Year 9 pupil made a BBC2 television documentary about the estate.
- A Japanese teacher spent nearly a month at Peers as part of an internship scheme.

The most recent outreach activity is an independent educational charity which recognises and supports parents as their children's first educators. The project has raised £1 million over a period of eighteen months and works with families by providing learning materials, organising local meetings for parents and advising parents how to prepare their children for school life.

Stages of Concern interviews

Seven members of staff, representative of a wide cross-section of job specifications and length of service in the school and in their profession, were interviewed during a two-day visit.

119

Mark: deputy headteacher

Mark is deputy headteacher and has been in this post for four years. His previous two appointments gave him experience as a head of subject and pastoral leader, and fitted him for the wide responsibilities he now carries. Until the beginning of the term in which he was interviewed, his main responsibilities, in addition to a 50 per cent teaching commitment, were for student issues, in particular where tutors and heads of year needed support, liaison with all other users of the campus, and marketing. He is editor of the school paper and responsible for other aspects of publicity. The appointment, for two terms, of the other deputy headteacher to the acting headship of a local middle school has given him in addition the latter's responsibilities for staffing and budgeting. Somehow he manages to combine these multifarious duties with part-time work for a Master's degree, researching into post-16 education.

His SoC profile (see Figure 8.1) is typical of a senior member of the staff and a high-flyer, ambitious for a headship in due course. Not unexpectedly, he has virtually no concerns in the first four elements of the histogram: even management, despite the heavy additional load he is carrying, is of low concern, probably because he, like a number of other staff, works until 7.30 pm on the school premises most days. His concern for students and for supporting and collaborating with staff is very high; he believes that this is the cornerstone of his job. He is full of developmental ideas for the school, covering the curriculum, outreach and opportunities for raising the prestige of Peers; as such, he is clearly a refocusing user.

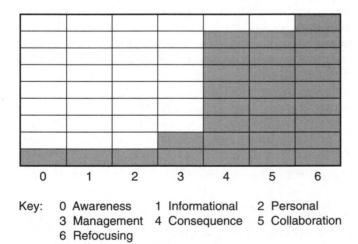

Key: 0 Awareness 1 Informational 2 Personal
      3 Management 4 Consequence 5 Collaboration
      6 Refocusing

Figure 8.1 Mark: deputy headteacher

Marion: school counsellor

Marion is the school counsellor. She began as a learning support assistant and, though not a qualified teacher, became a counsellor when the previous incumbent left. Her work is multi-faceted. She works with individual students where there is family crisis, on a short-term basis to avoid dependency, seeing them for one lesson a week. She sees herself as the link between staff and students, in particular over those with attendance problems, meeting weekly with heads of year over long-term refusers and those who have difficulty in coming to school. Her strategies include a daily phone call to as many as twelve students in each year group of compulsory schooling. Her key aim is to help young people to help themselves.

She is much involved with parents. Mothers come readily to see her either because she invites them or of their own volition when they have problems: 'Because I am not a teacher, the families see me as a link.' An important element of her work is to support Year 12 pupils, particularly those of lower ability who stay on for the Diploma in Vocational Education. She is a member of the strong sixth-form team, the support and control of which is, for many students, crucial to their success. The ethos of the school at this level, as she sees it, is that it has 'a new start and [staff] are nagged to carry it through!'

She is responsible for referrals, to general practitioners, social services, the adolescent psychiatric unit, always in consultation with tutors and year heads where this is possible. With this workload it is surprising that she does not rate management concern more highly (see Figure 8.2).

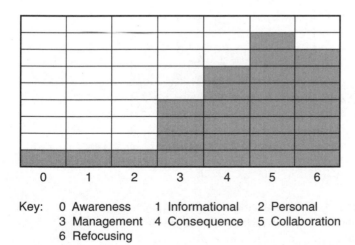

Key: 0 Awareness   1 Informational   2 Personal
      3 Management   4 Consequence   5 Collaboration
      6 Refocusing

Figure 8.2   Marion: school counsellor

Her high level in refocusing arises from her conviction that, in her field of work, flexibility is essential. She finds herself repeatedly saying: 'Is there another way of doing things?'

She is also an active parent governor. Her election is a clear indication of the trust that parents have in her work and the caring systems that she has evolved.

Nancy: coordinator for geography

Nancy realised that this was the school in which she wanted eventually to teach when she heard the headteacher talk to university PGCE students about the Tanzania link. In 1995 she was appointed to the post of coordinator for geography at Peers.

The students were, not surprisingly in the light of the school's philosophy, very different from those of her previous school: more forward, quite capable of describing in forthright terms a lesson that they found boring, but equally prepared to discuss why it was so and to accept her argument that, while she tried to make all lessons interesting and dynamic, there are aspects of the National Curriculum which do not lend themselves to such an approach.

She has ideas as a tutor of what more might be done, but accepts that geography must be her present priority, particularly as she was preparing to pilot the new GNVQ syllabus for non-advanced level students. Accepting that her high task concern is a consequence of her relative newness as a staff member of Peer School, she is well on the way to being a refocusing user (see Figure 8.3).

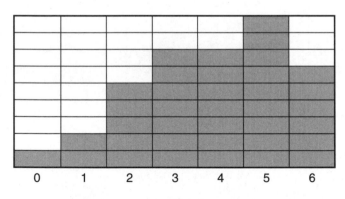

Key: 0 Awareness   1 Informational   2 Personal
      3 Management   4 Consequence   5 Collaboration
      6 Refocusing

Figure 8.3 Nancy: NQT and coordinator for geography

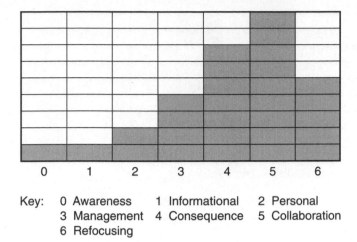

Key: 0 Awareness   1 Informational   2 Personal
      3 Management   4 Consequence   5 Collaboration
      6 Refocusing

Figure 8.4   Olive: coordinator for art with 30 years' experience

Olive: coordinator for art

Olive is one of several teachers interviewed who have taught on the campus for several decades, thirty years in her case. She experienced amalgamation of the selective and non-selective schools, and age-group changes, and has served under the four headteachers of Peers since 1969. As coordinator for art she is responsible for one of the school's most interesting areas, as the displays around the school and the portfolios of examination work being assembled at the time of the author's visit demonstrated.

She was clearly committed to the ethos of the school and the oppor-tunities it gave her to transmit her skills and to run an influential department. Her profile (Figure 8.4), as with most of the staff, showed relatively low management concern, but was high on consequence for students and on collaboration with staff. Refocusing was, in her view, not a major concern, and mostly concerned internal departmental developments rather than initiatives for change within the school as a whole.

Norman: head of languages

Norman has taught on the campus for twenty-three years, having begun as the teacher of Latin in the selective school. He is now head of languages. Latin has long since disappeared from the main curriculum, although it was offered in 1993–94 in the 'twilight' session, and two pupils who had continued to study the subject privately for the next two years passed Latin GCSE in 1996.

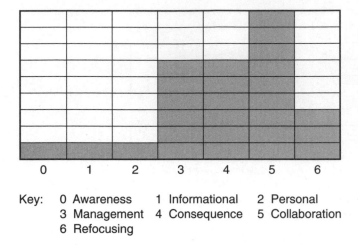

Key: 0 Awareness   1 Informational   2 Personal
      3 Management 4 Consequence   5 Collaboration
      6 Refocusing

Figure 8.5   Norman: head of languages with 23 years' experience

French and German are the two languages currently taught in the school. French is taught to all Year 9 students, continues as a GCSE option in the next two years and is offered at A level. From September 1996 the National Curriculum required a modern language to be taken by all pupils of statutory school age to the end of Year 11. German features in the 'twilight' session, in particular to enable some pupils to take two modern languages.

Norman is remarkably sanguine about tackling the problems of teaching a modern language to low achievers beyond Year 9. He values the 'twilight' session as an expedient for 'putting a quart in a pint pot', but regrets that pupils and staff may not be able to give of their best after a long day.

His SoC profile (Figure 8.5) shows him as being more concerned over management issues than he would normally expect to be, largely because of the change imposed by the National Curriculum. He claims to have little interest in refocusing, being content 'to plough his own furrow'! On the other hand his collaboration with staff is very high, as was evidenced by his involvement in staffroom discussions on pupils, developments and activities.

Peter: head of physics

Peter has been at the school for seven years as head of physics and coordinator of Year 10. Although his managerial responsibility is considerable, he does not regard himself as unduly pressured, as his 'task' concern indicates (Figure 8.6). He has willingly taken on a major extra-curricular role, and his contribution to the international perspectives of staff and students has been broadened through the Tanzania link: he was one of the key

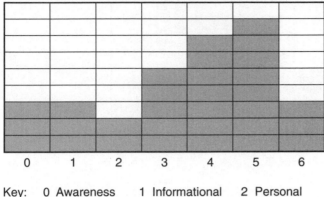

Key: 0 Awareness   1 Informational   2 Personal
      3 Management   4 Consequence   5 Collaboration
      6 Refocusing

Figure 8.6 Peter: head of physics with 7 years' experience

organisers for the 1993 and 1995 visits to Katumba. He enthused at length about this project which he regards as vital to the promotion of international understanding. His SoC profile is one that shows no particular concern for refocusing but, like many of his colleagues, is very high on pupil consequences and staff collaboration.

Richard: DVE and careers

Richard is another of those with a long experience in schools on the campus. In twenty-seven years he has served through a number of amalgamations and 'many headteachers, all with very different ideas of how to run a school'. He operates within the English department, but his key involvements are with the Diploma in Vocational Education (DVE) and, pre-eminently, with careers. He is clearly an able systems' man; he has placements available with 350 employers, and matching pupils to employers is now computerised, much enhanced by the installation of the new computer system. He is well supported by tutors, who readily visit their 'placed' students and who often deal with 'first-line' problems, 'of which there are very few', he hastened to add. In his view, careers advice and work-experience placements are so well organised that he has no management concern worth mentioning: 'This is not a boast, simply that I have been doing this job for a long time and all the paperwork and other details are so well established that they are virtually automatic.'

He rates staff collaboration and student consequences as highly as any member of staff (Figure 8.7). It is worthy of note that, while the interview

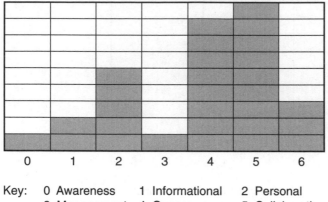

Key: 0 Awareness   1 Informational   2 Personal
       3 Management   4 Consequence   5 Collaboration
       6 Refocusing

Figure 8.7   Richard: DVE and careers with 25 years' experience

was taking place, DVE students were coming and going, completing final assignments, entirely self-possessed and mannerly, and working with praiseworthy independence.

General

The scattergram (Figure 8.8) shows a remarkably low level of awareness (0) and informational (1) concerns. This is true also of personal (2) concerns, particularly when one observes that one of the two teachers who rated moderately highly was relatively new to the school, and the other spoke extensively in his interview about his prospects for early retirement. Management (3) was the most variable of the concerns. The interviews suggested that the management pressures on staff were evident but only intermittent. However, the interviews took place at the time when public examinations were looming and when pupils were showing some understandable tension, requiring of staff a greater level than usual of pastoral care. Consequence (4) and collaboration (5) were remarkably high, echoing the evidence from the interviews that communication and collegiality are the key indicators of the success of this school. The author urged interviewees to be scrupulous in their self-assessment in these two concerns in particular; all were sure that these fairly represented their status. Two staff showed clear indications of being renewing users. One, the deputy headteacher, as the interview record indicates, undertook joint responsibility with the headteacher for major developments of school policy and planning.

0	1	2	3	4	5	6
					****	*
				**	***	
			*	***		*
			*	**		*
		**	*			*
			**			
*	*					***
	**	**	*			
******	****	***	*			

Key: 0 Awareness 1 Informational 2 Personal
3 Management 4 Consequence 5 Collaboration
6 Refocusing

Figure 8.8 Peers School scattergram

Summary

Leadership, not only from the headteacher and the senior teaching staff but at all levels of staff, both teaching and non-teaching, is one of the most evident features of this school. Communication, formal and informal, but particularly the latter, is undoubtedly the key to successful leadership in Peers. Developmental ideas are accepted for consideration from whatever source they come, and proposals from the senior management are given detailed study at all staff levels before implementation.

The staffroom is often the ideal place in which to observe the spirit of a school. Staff talked about pupil behaviour or curriculum development as readily as about the staff and senior pupils' visit to a London theatre the previous night. There is no sense of hurry to be gone; meetings take place and individual staff can be seen talking to pupils after school ends. The headteacher and other senior staff take their turn in supervising morning break and the lunch hour, and set an example that staff readily follow over dealing with any pupil or parent issue as soon as humanly possible.

In an upper school, the focus on teaching and learning will inevitably be oriented mainly towards examination and diploma success. It is in the range of what is offered that this school demonstrates its concern to make both teaching and learning match the potentiality of its pupils, perhaps most evidently in the City and Guilds Intermediate Diploma of Vocational Education available to post-16 students and in the introduction, in September 1996, of foundation and intermediate GNVQ courses in art and design, business, and health and social care.

Assessment procedures demonstrate the school's belief, highlighted in the prospectus, that 'assessment is central to the teaching and learning in every area of the curriculum'.

For a school which draws its pupils mainly from the housing estate in which it is sited, pupil achievement in 1996 of 26 per cent A–C grades at General Certificate in Secondary Education is reasonable, given that one-third of the pupils are regarded as having special needs. The performance of 16–18 year-old pupils taking the intermediate vocational qualification, where the thirty-nine entrants achieved a pass rate of 82 per cent, was the best in the LEA. Results seem set to improve, as the school is increasingly proving attractive to entrants from the city as a whole in Year 9 and Year 11. The attitude of staff to pupils is one of 'you can do it!', whatever the endeavour: academic, sporting, artistic, or coping with difficult domestic situations.

It would be surprising if, in an upper school, every effort were not made to place the responsibility for learning on the pupils themselves. However, home conditions are not always such as to provide the facilities, or even to encourage and understand the need, for self-study out of school hours. The study support centre is therefore a valuable support for such pupils, as is the on-campus community library, which is becoming, through the school's 'technology college' designation, a computerised information and literacy centre.

The many extra-curricular activities are one indication of the participation of pupils in the life of the school: drama, music, art and craft, the Tanzanian link, for example. Less apparently relevant is the close relationship between staff and pupils, the outcome of which is that they are involved in their own self-development and therefore better able to participate in the adult world for which they are being prepared.

A formal system of rewards and incentives is not within the school's philosophy: such systems serve, so staff hold, to differentiate students by commending some at the expense of others. The incentives lie in the constant encouragement given by tutors to all the pupils in their tutor group, and the recognition that what matters is that all students measure their perfor-mance and development against their potential.

Parents are involved both formally, through the activities of the Friends of the School, and by the open-access policy described in the prospectus: 'There are regular report and consultation evenings, but parents are encour-aged to get in touch at any time.' Parents of absentees are contacted routinely, and any incident leads to an immediate request that they visit the school as soon as possible to discuss the matter.

9

RISCA COMPREHENSIVE
SCHOOL

Introduction

When the headteacher took over Risca Comprehensive School in January 1994, she found a demoralised and disillusioned staff. The number on roll in a school opened in 1977 for 1,000 pupils was now under 650, partly in consequence of demographic changes, but more particularly of the accessibility for parental choice of the only GM school in Wales and of a second comprehensive school, still known locally to many as 'the Grammar'.

In her first few months in the school she was quickly made aware of staff attitudes that were contributing to poor standards of pupil performance and a *laissez-faire* ambience.

Although the National Curriculum was then well established in Wales, it had not led to any changes in the school curriculum, which included road-traffic education, child care for girls and motor-vehicle maintenance for boys. The total of twenty-five hours of lessons in a week required by the Education Act was not being observed.

When the present headteacher was appointed, she was told by the governors that the school had £10,000 remaining in its budget. She was soon to learn from the LEA that, instead, it had a deficit budget of £86,000 which it was her immediate responsibility to eliminate. The school was overstaffed and in the next two years redundancy agreements for eight staff and appointments to other schools saw some of the staff depart. Symptomatic of early attitudes was the class teacher's response, audible to the class, to her enquiry 'How are they doing?': 'Not bad, considering how thick they are'. At the next staff meeting the headteacher made it clear that all children in this school must be valued.

Developments in organisation and management

One of the earliest changes was the introduction of clearly defined job descriptions. In normal circumstances the headteacher would have involved members of staff in the writing of their own, but urgency, and their lack

129

of any experience of management processes, led to the responsibility falling on her. She created model roles for subject teachers and pastoral coordinators, for example she documented the role of the newly established senior management team and allocated to the five members – the two deputy headteachers, two senior teachers and herself – specific responsibilities.

In 1993 the school had been awarded, on the basis of an LEA-supported application, funding from the Technology Schools Initiative. It was now the headteacher's responsibility to put the money to good use in curricular development. The curriculum summary for 1995–96 shows that, for Year 10, the two open-option blocks had been extended to include a double-option leading to the GNVQ and the humanities extended to offer sociology and business studies. Double balanced science had also been introduced and, by now, Welsh was taught to all classes up to Year 9 and then as an option subject, in preparation for its compulsory inclusion in the Welsh National Curriculum from 1996–97. The curriculum summary for 1996–97 was prepared and published to staff two terms in advance; a marked change from previous practice.

The staff is now organised into five faculties, with, in addition, a full-time learning-support teacher. The pastoral system is year-based, with a coordinator for Year 7, one for Years 8 and 9, and one for Years 10 and 11. This organisation of staff enabled the headteacher to produce for the school year 1994–95 the first school development plan that the school had known. Each priority followed the established rubric of: target, purpose (why? for whom? for what?), success criteria, strengths and needs, action (with key dates) and review procedures. The core elements of the first school development plan were to raise pupil aspirations through

- introducing records of achievement;
- improving teaching and learning styles;
- improving pupil involvement in school decision making; and
- integrating pupils with special educational needs.

Underpinning this and future school development plans was the succinct mission statement: 'To raise standards in all aspects of school life.'

For 1995–96 this meant continued detailed consideration of the curriculum, arriving at procedures for monitoring the delivery of the curriculum and pupil achievement, staffing issues, and the school environment.

Staffing

For 1995–96 there were 34.9 teaching staff and a total of 5.5 ancillary staff. With the development of the library as a major learning resource, a library technician was appointed for 1996–97. The budget now shows a healthy balance and the headteacher is discussing at senior management level where ancillary staffing might be increased to take more of the administrative load off teaching staff.

The staff profile had become somewhat atypical. There was a considerable age-gap between the very experienced teachers who stayed on and the newly qualified teachers appointed to replace those who had left on redundancy or to new posts.

Staff development was rationalised to meet school needs as set out in the school development plan. Previously staff had decided when they wished to do a particular in-service course; now the school needs and the budget allocation for staff development decide whether such needs should and can be met, the main determinant being the benefit to the school. The content of INSET days is defined at the beginning of each school year. Currently two of the five are allocated for the inter-school subject panels and one for joint training with the feeder primary schools. The other two are determined on the basis of school development plan priorities. For 1994–95, when for the first time all teachers became tutors, personal and social education was the priority; for 1995–96, it was training for the forthcoming OFSTED inspection. Much staff development takes place in staff meetings, the calendar for which is published annually. One innovation has been the allocation of individual middle-managers on a short-term basis to specific tasks. On my tour of the school I observed one head of department working voluntarily with the timetabling team to gain experience of the issues faced in this exercise. Another in-service strategy has been the attachment, for one half-term, to the senior management team of each of the five heads of faculty in turn. This is not only a learning process for those who might wish to apply for more senior posts but a means of creating a channel of communication between the senior management team and the teaching staff.

Teacher appraisal had not been introduced into the school by the previous headteacher, although by 1993 it had long been obligatory. Nor was the new headteacher able to introduce it when she was appointed, since at that time she was the only member of staff trained to carry out appraisals and there were other, more immediate, needs for in-service training. To date, her personal overseeing of the development of all staff and her frequent classroom observation have had to suffice. This is not a substitute for the devolved responsibility built into the appraisal process, and, with one deputy head now able to appraise, a start was made in the year beginning September 1996 with heads of faculty.

Parents

A significant change has taken place in the relationship between parents and the school. They now know that they can come freely to the school to discuss problems, often with the headteacher herself – since this is their expectation – but increasingly with either deputy. The development of the library – an inhospitable place where pupils could skulk unobserved and where the book stock was outdated and in poor repair – provided an opportunity for parents to assist in the reorganisation. Parents recognise that the redecoration of the school, an early priority as soon as the budget allowed, has made it a much more welcoming place. Breezeblock walls cannot readily be made attractive, but displays of pupils' work and large-scale murals on wooden frames have done much to break up stark corridors. All classrooms now have blackout, whiteboards and full carpeting. As has often been said by parents: 'Our children are beginning to feel proud of their school.'

Previously homework had been voluntary. Because children were not allowed to take books home, even the most committed rarely did any. Now it is compulsory and most parents have approved of the change since they recognise that it means greater opportunity for their children's academic achievement. The parents of children with learning difficulties have been heartened by the replacement of the remedial class – with children from Year 7 to Year 11 in the one unit – by learning support from a teacher who works alongside classroom teachers and through individual withdrawals.

Parents are undoubtedly becoming partners, but are reportedly still too lax in fulfilling their responsibilities to their children and the school. In 1994–95 the total absence rate was 12.6 per cent, and unauthorised absence was 2.3 per cent. 1995–96 figures showed some, but insufficient, improvement. The headteacher regards this as unacceptable. Parents echo those in the neighbourhood primary school, who say: 'So long as she/he is happy. . . . ' To those parents, and to staff who say that change is taking place too rapidly, she retorts: 'For these children this is their only chance.'

The school prospectus for parents is excellently informative, well set-out, and specific about parental responsibility for attendance, dress and their children's behaviour.

Governors

While some governors are highly supportive, there is a need for the governing body as a whole to be more pro-active. Until 1995 there was no curriculum committee. The headteacher is left to write the minutes, though this should be the responsibility of someone other than her, appointed by the governing body. Some attend school events regularly, others are seldom to be seen.

Stages of Concern interviews

Seven teachers and one technician were interviewed. As will be seen, for a majority of the teachers this had been the only school at which they had taught, and three had been at Risca Comprehensive School for twenty years or more. It is worthy of note that all the present staff appear to have adapted to a leadership style fundamentally different from that of the incumbent's predecessor and a rate of change that might have been considered impossible of achievement.

Carole: deputy head

Carole joined the staff in 1991, having had a wide experience of management posts in several Gwent schools. She was senior mistress of Cwm Carn Comprehensive School, but left it as a matter of principle when it became the first, and only, grant-maintained school in Wales.

She welcomed the possibility of radical change that the advent of a new headteacher appeared to offer. The role of deputy head that evolved to suit the needs of a rapidly evolving management system was symbiotic: the two deputy heads are jointly responsible for a wide range of management tasks set out in their common job specification. The purpose of this is clearly to encourage the interchange of tasks where this is beneficial to their personal development and to indicate to other members of the senior management team and the staff as a whole that, together with the headteacher, their concern is for whole-school development. The one differentiation is that one deputy head is responsible for KS3, including primary continuity, and the other for KS4, including tertiary continuity.

The heavy work-load undertaken by Carole does not seem in any way to deter her and it is evident that she works whatever hours the job requires. She recognises that the rate of change since 1994 was costly in terms of time and energy, but is well aware how easily change can become the status quo if the dynamic is not maintained. She believes, however, that there is

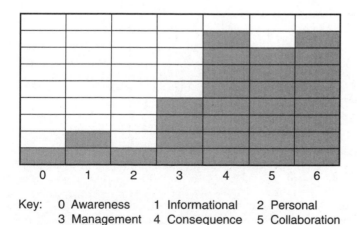

Key: 0 Awareness   1 Informational   2 Personal
       3 Management   4 Consequence   5 Collaboration
       6 Refocusing

Figure 9.1   Carole: deputy head

now a major role for the senior management team to bed down the change that has taken place in so short a time, without any loss of vision for the future development of the school.

Her SoC interview shows her to be a renewing user (Figure 9.1), and bears out the headteacher's view that she will soon be ready for promotion.

Gareth: head of technology

Risca Comprehensive School is the only school Gareth has taught in during more than twenty years in the profession. He is now head of the technology faculty, responsible for the coordination of the newly introduced GNVQ at foundation and intermediate levels. While he is professionally pleased with the new curricular opportunities before him, he admits, not surprisingly, that the rate of change under the new headteacher has been 'more than one can really cope with'. He recognises nevertheless that the level at which the school was working, particularly in the field of his own specialism, required 'change that was fundamental rather than evolutionary'. He now looks to a period of stability so that the changes can be consolidated.

On the positive side, there is a wealth of new equipment in the school to enable him to develop technology and to make the school more attractive when parents and children interested in this field make their selection of secondary school. Negatively, the high levels of informational and personal concern in the histogram (Figure 9.2) indicate serious doubts about his own capacity to cope with change. In interview he presented himself as someone reluctant to disclose that he needed strong support if he is to deliver what the senior management team expects of him.

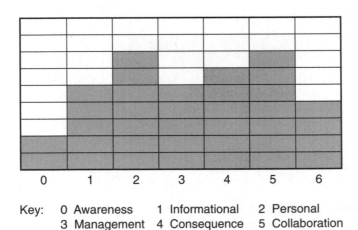

Key: 0 Awareness   1 Informational   2 Personal
       3 Management   4 Consequence   5 Collaboration
       6 Refocusing

Figure 9.2   Gareth: head of technology with 20 years' experience

Diane: Year-8 group tutor

Diane is a late entrant to the teaching profession, having trained at a Welsh college of education after her children were established in school. Her previous experience as a secretary and personnel officer made English an obvious choice for her specialism. Although her training was for the 8–13 age-group, her interest was in Years 7–11 and she was appointed to Risca in 1991. She is enthusiastic about the changes that have taken place since 1994:

> There is far more cohesion in curricular policy and the children are increasingly aware that change has been for their benefit. Some parents have been dubious, but there is a growing general approval.

The structuring of tutor groups is, she maintains, one of the key factors in school improvement. She is at present tutor to a Year-8 group and will remain with them throughout their time at the school. This gives her sustained contact with the parents. The second significant benefit for her of the restructuring of the school management has been the opportunity to develop significantly her collaboration with other members of staff. She admits to being fortunate here in that her head of faculty is highly approachable and supportive. Her SoC profile (Figure 9.3) is that of a well-established and experienced teacher, with few self-concerns.

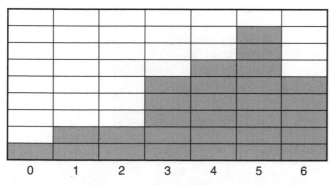

Key: 0 Awareness 1 Informational 2 Personal
3 Management 4 Consequence 5 Collaboration
6 Refocusing

Figure 9.3 Diane: mature NQT and Year-8 group tutor

Hugh: head of expressive arts

Hugh came to the school in 1991 as head of music and was appointed head of the faculty of expressive arts by the present headteacher when she reorganised the senior curriculum management into five faculties. The arts in general, and music in particular, had in his opinion been much neglected under the previous administration. The capitation allowance for his subject was a fixed figure and did nothing to enable him to develop his subject.

The present headteacher has, he emphasised, a positive and supportive attitude to the range of subjects for which he is now responsible. Budget planning is by submission to the senior management team of a statement of needs. The team looks at his claim and, where it feels that it cannot, at any rate at present, support the claim in full, he, like any other head of faculty, is called in to hear the reasons and, if he can, to modify the team's decision. This, he maintains, makes him a partner in decision making and enables him to present his colleagues in the faculty with a reasoned argument why their requests may not have been met in full.

His teaching accommodation has been much improved and development funding, as distinct from capitation, has enabled art, music and the recent introduction into the curriculum of drama to cover a wider range of activities than ever before. He found his half a term on attachment to the senior management team most valuable: 'I hadn't realised that there were so many things going on.' The introduction into the staff meetings' calendar of regular faculty meetings has, he maintains, developed a strong sense of collegiality among staff, and he is able to engage in corporate planning with his team.

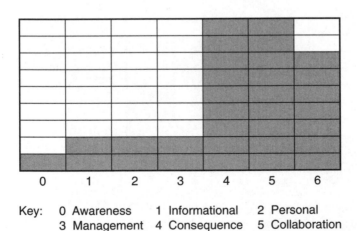

Key: 0 Awareness 1 Informational 2 Personal
      3 Management 4 Consequence 5 Collaboration
      6 Refocusing

Figure 9.4   Hugh: head of expressive arts

His SoC profile (Figure 9.4) shows him to be a highly experienced teacher, well on the way to being a renewing user.

Ellen: laboratory technician

Ellen came to the school in 1989 as laboratory technician responsible for the upkeep of the five science laboratories. She had left school after O levels and had taken an A level later. While in post she had taken the appropriate technician RSA examinations at both level 1 and level 2.

For her the greatest benefits of the new administration had been the introduction of the school day of five one-hour lessons. She described with good humour her former helter-skelter existence as she had to ferry apparatus and materials from store to laboratory and back again for shorter lessons and, though not a qualified teacher, she recognised the merits of the balanced science curriculum that had been introduced.

Her SoC profile (Figure 9.5) is interesting in that she stands very high on collaboration, finding herself now in a much better relationship with all staff. She appreciates the benefits for the students of the improved facilities and opportunities in science. Her somewhat high self-concern over information she explains by saying:

> I have all the information I need to know for my job, but I would say that there are aspects of the management of the school as a whole that I am not aware of. However, I have only to ask if there is anything I want to know.

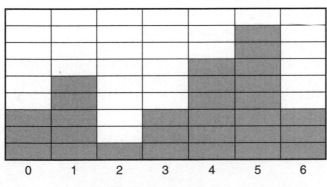

Key: 0 Awareness 1 Informational 2 Personal
      3 Management 4 Consequence 5 Collaboration
      6 Refocusing

Figure 9.5 Ellen: laboratory technician

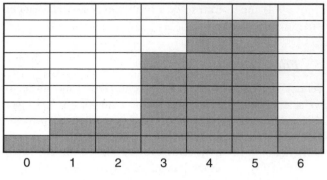

Key: 0 Awareness   1 Informational   2 Personal
      3 Management   4 Consequence   5 Collaboration
      6 Refocusing

Figure 9.6   Ian: coordinator for pastoral studies with 20 years' experience

Ian: coordinator for pastoral studies

Ian qualified as a teacher of sociology and joined the staff over twenty years ago:

> I have to say that until recently I had been growing more and more concerned about the *laissez-faire* attitude to management. Decisions were taken by vote in full staff meetings; that is not effective leadership, since people all too often vote on insufficient information and from self-interest. For years I was pushing for change. Nobody seemed to recognise that we had problems. Nothing of importance was ever addressed. As a school, we stagnated.

He is now coordinator for pastoral studies and feels that he is in a growth phase, both within the school and personally. He is studying for a Master's degree in his spare time, of which he admits without rancour that there is very little, since there is so much to do in the school. His SoC profile (Figure 9.6) is that of an experienced teacher with few self-concerns, but highly committed to the first two elements of 'impact' consequence for students and collaboration with staff.

Jeremy: head of art

Jeremy was another of those who had been at the school for over twenty years. He was one of two teachers of art and, when in 1994 the present headteacher found the school budget necessitated substantial reductions in staffing, it was his colleague who took retirement under the redundancy provision: 'We got on well as colleagues, but one of us had to go.'

Jeremy was made head of department and immediately set about transforming the curriculum to meet the requirements of the National Curriculum. He seems to have enjoyed the challenge of major change that was required. The organisation of materials was non-existent. The art room needed to be completely reorganised to provide the opportunities for pupils to do the full range of work in the subject. He devised and implemented programmes of study.

He covers the art teaching for all classes, except for some help from the textile teacher. He has misgivings about changes in the planning for the 1996–97 Year 10 option-blocks, which has reduced the opportunity for pupils to take his subject, while at the same time giving him a class of thirty in the one option-block where art continues. He is aware that procedures exist through his head of faculty for raising the need for this to be modified, if not for the year immediately coming, then for the future.

His SoC profile (Figure 9.7) was initially remarkable for the high level of management concern, which seems to run counter to the confidence he evinced in his planning and management of change. Pressed on this, he felt that there was a need for consolidation in the school as a whole, and the level reflects the overall situation, as he saw it, rather than his own area of management. Realising this, he modified his own level of concern to point 6. The same might well be true of his relatively high personal concern, since he was obviously feeling aggrieved by the present status of art as a

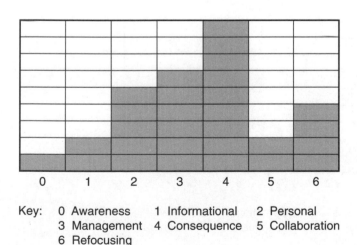

0 1 2 3 4 5 6

Key: 0 Awareness   1 Informational   2 Personal
      3 Management   4 Consequence   5 Collaboration
      6 Refocusing

Figure 9.7   Jeremy: head of art with 20 years' experience

GCSE subject and the size of the Year 10 class for 1996–97. However, he was adamant that this should remain as it stood.

Keith: head of communications

Keith was a comparatively recent arrival, having joined the staff in 1991 as head of modern languages, and having been promoted in 1994 to head of the communications faculty, with overall responsibility for French, German, Welsh and English.

The introduction of Welsh, required under the National Curriculum, presents some problems in a non-Welsh speaking area, and he was particularly pleased that some pupils had successfully offered the subject at GCSE through the option programme. He applauded the parity given to German and French up to the end of Year 9, and looked for improvement in pupil achievement in GCSE in their chosen language or languages as the grounding in the subjects improved. He was in no doubt about the need for change:

> The rate of change was rapid, but essential. Those, like me, who had come from other schools were aware of the need for change, but some members of staff were clearly disturbed. We are now entering a more stable phase.

His SoC profile (Figure 9.8) shows particularly high concerns for pupil achievement and collaboration with colleagues.

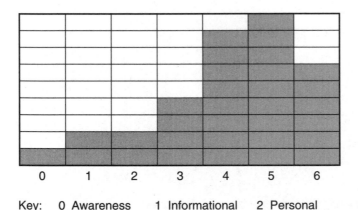

Key: 0 Awareness   1 Informational   2 Personal
        3 Management 4 Consequence 5 Collaboration
        6 Refocusing

Figure 9.8 Keith: head of communications

General

The scattergram (Figure 9.9) demonstrates that the sample of staff interviewed are low in self-concerns, and, with one apparent exception, in personal (2) concerns. Management (3) concerns exist, for individuals and possibly also for the school as a whole, but the profile would doubtless be accepted by the headteacher as satisfactory in the light of her need to restructure rapidly to make the school effective. Consequence (4) and collaboration (5) are encouragingly high. The spread in refocusing (6) shows that there is among some staff the willingness and ability to support change directly.

Summary

The headteacher's leadership was initially, of necessity, because of low staff morale and public esteem, Bourbon in style (Nias 1980) and a combination of 'tells' and 'sells'. Within three years, with retirements, redundancies, internal promotions to new management posts and new appointments, the strong positive leadership was becoming a feature of staff collegiality. The curriculum has been a key priority and the standards of teaching and learning have been under close scrutiny and have developed admirably. Assessment procedures were previously largely non-existent, and recording class and individual progress is now well in place. Expectations of pupil achievement are growing rapidly, but entrenched staff and pupil attitudes are not eradicated overnight. On the other hand, pupil motivation is as yet not high, and there seems to be insufficient realisation among many that they have a part to play in the learning process.

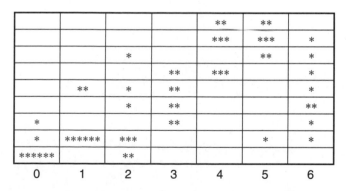

0	1	2	3	4	5	6
				**	**	
				***	***	*
		*			**	*
			**	***		*
	**	*	**			*
		*	**			**
*			**			*
*	******	***			*	*
******		**				

Key: 0 Awareness   1 Informational   2 Personal
3 Management   4 Consequence   5 Collaboration
6 Refocusing

Figure 9.9   Risca Comprehensive School scattergram

The incentives for pupils to succeed are largely through the improving success rate in examinations which undoubtedly provides younger pupils with a feeling that they too can be achievers. The extended range of areas of study, in particular GNVQ, is a further incentive.

The physical environment has much improved over the past few years and there are indications of greater parental support and involvement. A more pro-active involvement of parents will take time to achieve. In 1994 the baseline for extra-curricular activities was abysmally low. They are now a strong growth point, particularly in the expressive arts, following recent appointments of a head of the expressive arts faculty and of an experienced drama teacher.

10

ASSESSING THE CASE
STUDIES

Introduction

It would be feasible to use Conley's dimensions of restructuring (see Conley 1993 and Table 3.1) as the basis for assessing the extent to which the case study schools had become restructured. However, while one accepts the value of the essential inter-relationship of the central, enabling and supporting variables, there is a difference between a 'road map to restructuring', as he calls it, and a means of analysing how far along the road the schools have progressed.

Before Conley's book was published in 1993, I had developed and used in training an extrapolation from the article by Corbett (1990) on roles, relationships, rules and results (see pp. 38–9) which provides a conceptual framework for analysis. The key features are shown in Table 10.1.

The study of restructuring described in this book started from a significantly different baseline in each of the case study schools. Two schools, one primary, one secondary, began to restructure from what might well be described as a zero base. The headteacher of the infants school had the advantage of several years' service in the school as deputy headteacher, which, frustrating though this must have been to someone with ideas of what was needed to make West Town Lane School an effective school, nevertheless gave her the opportunity of an in-depth study of its needs. The headteacher of Risca Comprehensive School was in a worse plight: some staff were mere time-servers, and others were in a state of limbo through lack of leadership. Fortunately for the school she did not hold back from strong leadership but instead began a thorough analysis of what was needed to make this school effective.

The headteachers of one primary school, Kates Hill, and one secondary school, Peers, have a very different history. Each had been in post for about ten years and in that time had introduced a pattern of leadership that is close to the 'invitational' model (p. 28) described by Stoll and Fink (1996), with its emphasis on personal qualities allied to professional support and encouragement. Both headteachers have been highly innovative, but have

Table 10.1   Framework for the analysis of restructuring

Roles	Leadership – governors
	The management structure
	Job specifications
	Boundary management
Relationships	Staff relationships
	Staff development
	Parental involvement
	Community perceptions
	Governor responsibilities
Rules	School policies
	Financial control
	Administration systems
Results	School development plan review
	Monitoring and evaluation
	Pupil performance
	Quality control

at the same time been at pains to underpin their transformational concepts by competent transactional measures.

The headteacher of the fifth school, Risca Primary School, might be thought also to have begun from a zero baseline, were it not that she had time, as the newly appointed headteacher of one of the schools to be closed and amalgamated into the new school, to make a thorough analysis of the transactional developments that would be needed for the new school to be effective. She had the added advantage of meeting most of her staff well in advance of the move, and of conveying to them her educational philosophy.

It will be apparent in the rest of this chapter that no school studied has restructured to an equal extent in all four sets of Corbett's analytical framework and their subsets, nor would this have been expected. Nevertheless, one of the principles of restructuring is that there is a need for constant self-monitoring lest any of its elements should ossify. In the sections which follow, the analysis deals with both primary and secondary schools and compares and contrasts the stage of development each has reached in different circumstances.

Roles

Leadership

The National Commission on Education in its report *Success Against the Odds* (1996) found that, pre-eminent among the features that characterise successful schools was strong positive leadership by the headteacher and senior staff. This view is reiterated in most of the literature on managerial leadership in schools over at least two decades. In all five schools leadership of this kind was undoubtedly a major factor in restructuring. However, the practical interpretation of leadership was significantly different in each case, designed to meet the current conditions. Nevertheless, there appears to have been a common assumption that the leadership of the principal, or the headteacher and senior staff, must, for the evolution of an effective school, be disseminated, at the appropriate stage of the school's development, to include all staff in collegiate decision making.

Leadership in the primary schools

In West Town Lane Infants School the headteacher's dynamism and determination were clearly the reason for the school's success in moving to considerable achievement. There was, therefore, a more overt centralisation of leadership than in the other two primary schools. Nevertheless, though developmental ideas stemmed from her views of what makes an effective school, there was full discussion within the management team and staff of how these ideas were to be implemented. The senior management team has now given place to a management team which includes non-post holders. For those not involved in the initial decision making, there is no lack of information or discussion on proposed developments.

One possible disadvantage of a small infants school like West Town Lane is that all members of staff, regardless of status, have to carry a number of management roles. Without the headteacher's perception of the developmental map of what can and should be done at what stage, there might well be a feeling among staff of overload, lack of direction and the imposition of excessively time-consuming tasks. The staff's awareness that their contribution to the map is valued raises their self-esteem and turns the disadvantage into advantage.

In Kates Hill Primary School there was leadership of a very different kind. The headteacher has taken the school over a period of ten years through a succession of innovations, all, she believes, interdependent and consonant with the restructuring of the school. She chose a role for herself that was not usual, in the Belbin (1981) terminology that of 'shaper', but that did not diminish her role as leader. From the outset of her headship there was an affirmation of her intention to develop corporate decision making. It is apparent that, to begin with, staff looked to her for leadership in the hierarchical mode, and from this she weaned them to a belief that they, particularly the senior management team, were also leaders. Each innovation was discussed at all levels of the staff, and while there is no instance of staff rejecting an innovation they certainly influenced decisions on the pace for its adoption.

With an open-door policy allied with her own openness, which led her constantly to sound out the reasons for problems and achievements, the headteacher developed among all staff corporate responsibility at a very high level, as was shown in the Stages of Concern interviews.

In September 1995 the headteacher was seconded for one academic year as an associate OFSTED inspector. An experienced headteacher was seconded to Kates Hill for this period. The interviews for the research here presented took place in the first month of his incumbency, and most senior staff expressed their enthusiasm about their ability to 'hold the fort' until the headteacher returned. Yet this euphoria did not last. It is no reflection on the ability of the temporary incumbent, whose management style no doubt met the needs of his own institution, but there began to be, towards the end of the first term, expressions of concern about lack of communication, and a number of problems began to surface.

Chance played a part in the events that followed. The serious illness of the deputy headteacher of the school from which the acting headteacher had come led the governing body of that school to require his return at the end of the spring term. The LEA replaced him in Kates Hill by seconding an experienced headteacher, formerly on the Kates Hill staff, who had turned her own school in two years from one listed by OFSTED at the time of her appointment as 'in need of special measures' to one deemed on re-inspection to be 'satisfactory to good'. Importantly, the staff had faith in her ability to put the management of the school on an even keel, pending the headteacher's return in September 1996.

What had occurred highlights the fragile nature of leadership when continuity is broken. While the circumstances which led to a decline in staff morale could not have been predicted with certainty, there is always the possibility that, when strong and effective leadership in a particular mode is withdrawn, there will be some deleterious impact on the effectiveness of the school.

Headteacher leadership at the third case study primary school, Risca Primary School, has been of yet another kind. The headteacher had previous, highly regarded, experience at this level in another LEA. There was evident much goodwill from the teachers who were transferred from the closing schools or were newly appointed. Above all, she had time to evaluate the needs of the new school and to set up an action plan in the short, medium and long term to structure its curricular and managerial development.

Much had happened in the interim between the opening of the school and my visits to interview the headteacher and a proportion of the staff. The headteacher has a clarity of purpose much welcomed by the staff. Teachers have taken on a considerable workload to produce, under her direction, policies for every aspect of the curriculum and the running of the school. They have valued the fact that she has encouraged them to set up working parties with colleagues of their choice, and, no less, her own involvement as critic, timekeeper and monitor.

146

There is more overt control from this headteacher than from the incumbent at Kates Hill. Interview data demonstrate that this was the need of the staff at the present stage of the school's development, in her opinion and in theirs. As staff gain confidence in what is, to all of them, a new management situation, one which seeks to empower them, they are taking on greater responsibility of their own accord. For some senior staff, used to a formal and hierarchical form of management, the present style is acknowledged to be a revelation and a liberation. In terms of personal relationships, the headteacher has demonstrated an openness of behaviour which is rapidly devolving to staff attitudes, both to each other and to pupils.

Leadership in the secondary schools

It is difficult to imagine leadership styles demonstrated in the two case-study secondary schools which, on the face of it, were so different, yet were equally effective. The headteacher of Risca Comprehensive School had been the key decision maker and has felt the need to have a high profile in directing the management of the school from the very first days of her appointment. The creation, for the first time, of an effective school management team and the empowerment of the newly created heads of faculty were recent stages of an ongoing process, and the success of senior and middle-management continues to demand of her the regular overseeing and constant encouragement of her teams. For her the key leadership skill lies in the perception of times at which she can safely ease herself out of a dominant leadership role, in the knowledge that other staff will make decisions that accord with the principles set out in the mission statement and the policy documents.

Innovative practices, such as the attachment in rotation of a middle-manager to the senior management team for half a term, are an encouragement to all staff to perceive that the school is not run by a cabal. In interview several staff made it clear that they had appreciated, and were living up to, the demands being made on them in their newly created job specifications. The headteacher appeared to be ready to move, as the opportunity presented itself, from a directive leadership role to an increasingly corporate management style.

The headteacher of Peers School had been in post for far longer than Risca's head. The changes that he had had to initiate in the early days after his appointment required more directive leadership than he now exercises. Nevertheless, his first step on arrival was to undertake a consultative exercise with all staff to ascertain what they regarded as the priorities in organisational and managerial change. The leadership now exercised at all levels and in so many fields of activity makes it difficult to evaluate the situation which he encountered nine years ago on his appointment, but it was clear that, whether or not the staff regarded his leadership then as directive, they now see themselves as a team in which all have the ability to contribute to the making of school policy, albeit within the framework of the headteacher's vision for the school.

A key attribute of effective leadership is high visibility. One of the first actions of the headteacher of Risca Comprehensive School was to remove the 'traffic lights' outside her door that indicated 'engaged', 'wait', 'come in'. She described this as inimical to easy relationships with staff, a status symbol with authoritarian overtones. Parents wanting to see her speak to the secretary, who makes a judgement on whether or not a deputy-head is available if the headteacher is not, and in every case ensures that a parent in urgent need is seen with the least delay. Staff find the headteacher readily accessible as she goes round the school corridors. Pupils approach her easily, and nothing is too trivial for her to listen to. This high visibility, staff reported, contrasts with the reclusive attitude of her predecessor. Importantly, it is a model of appropriate leadership for all staff.

The headteacher of Peers School similarly rated high visibility as crucial to his concept of leadership. He too was around the school as much as possible. In addition, he took on duties, such as supervision of the tuck shop during morning break, partly so that he could be approachable to students, but equally so that he could be seen by staff to bear some of their load of trivial but necessary tasks.

His office had a picture window occupying most of the wall overlooking one of the busy pupil routes during lesson changes. Another headteacher might well have installed curtains, but he made a point of facing the window during conversation with a visitor, making a mental note of anything amiss, and dealing with the incident himself later *and* informing the appropriate tutor if the incident was anything more than trivial. Thus he demonstrated proactive leadership without overriding the authority of the pastoral staff. His interest was not only 'disciplinary', however.

The management structure

In all five schools the management structure has much in common with that of any good school. First, the headteacher had definitive responsibility, to governors, parents and pupils, for curriculum development, pupil progress, sound financial management and the implementation of national and local policies. Second, the management team was routinely consulted over each development in the school's action plan and in the regular assessment of the efficacy of past decisions. Its members' experience was valued and their advice heeded, and they took on short-term tasks beyond their job specifications to contribute to the monitoring of progress. Finally, the structure has been designed to devolve tasks to teachers outside the management team, partly as a means of staff development but above all because no school today can run effectively without the active involvement in management of all its staff. In two of the three primary schools a relatively flat management structure has been developed in a very short time, despite the lack of any previous history of corporate management. Interview evidence suggests that almost all staff were happy with the managerial experience they were acquiring.

Kates Hill, however, had broken new ground in redefining roles: boundary manager, resource manager, special needs/personnel manager and quality manager (see pp. 86–8 for responsibilities). That the headteacher undertook the first role was understandable since this was central to the school's purpose. Thereafter, while initially the remaining three roles were allocated to incumbents according to their interests and abilities, when a vacancy arises the post is filled by someone with the skills to take on these responsibilities. Thus, on the appointment of the first quality controller to the deputy headship of another school, the post was filled internally by a member of staff who had shown considerable interest and expertise in this field.

The membership and roles of the Kates Hill senior management team may well be unique. However, when the opportunity arises in any school, usually through staff promotions and retirements, a reconsideration of who does what in the senior management team might well be undertaken to bring it more into line, if need be, with the current requirements for effective learning.

In both secondary schools, and for different reasons, the incoming head-teacher had the task of establishing a suitable management structure in as short a time as possible. Peers School was faced with the task of adapting immediately to the demands of preparing for the implementation of the National Curriculum. The implications for a school which had previously operated a modular curriculum, and had structured staff teams in order to deliver that curriculum, were considerable. By 1994, under the previous regime, Risca Comprehensive School had not yet adapted to the demands of the curricula of Key Stages 3 and 4. For quite different reasons, there-fore, radical change in the management structure of both schools was a matter of urgency.

In both schools the requirements of local financial management assisted this change in a way which might normally have been deemed undesirable. School rolls determine school budgets and both schools had suffered a decline in pupil numbers. There was a need, over a period of several years, for retrenchment to be made, largely through redundancies, until the budget could be balanced. Yet the departure through early retirement of a number of senior staff opened up in each school the possibility of rapid change in the management structure. In the main, reorganisation was achieved through the internal appointment of staff who had the potential to manage a faculty or pastoral structure.

Job specifications

While job specifications were a required part of the working literature of all schools, there remained two tendencies which militated against effective restructuring. The first was for the school to consider the specification as 'a tablet of stone'. A review of specifications should be among the processes that each school should undertake routinely if it is to become a self-monitoring organisation (White and Poster 1997). There are in any school possibilities of changes that arise from developments within the curriculum or the management system. There was also the important consideration that the in-service training of teachers may sometimes be better effected by changes in their areas of responsibility than by attendance at courses. Sometimes changes take place almost imperceptibly, and job specifications may no longer relate to what a particular teacher is currently responsible for.

In West Town Lane and the two Risca schools the immediate task was to create the job specifications of existing staff, since no such documentation had existed before. In primary schools, where every teacher must be a coordinator of a curriculum area, of a key stage, or of an area such as INSET, and in addition someone must be found to take additional responsibility for the library, health and safety, displays, extra-curricular activities (the list seems endless), there may be a tendency to leave well alone. This would not be effective management. Reviews of job specifications may have indicated that changes would be beneficial to the school, or the individual, or both.

It is important that all other stakeholders – students, governors, parents – are aware in broad outline of the parameters of job specifications, at least to the extent of being able to ask any member of staff, teaching or ancillary, to whom to go for help or information. In Risca Comprehensive School it was clear that, while students seem to have this understanding, many parents and governors do not. With its longer history of effective management, it was evident that at Peers School a high level of understanding of roles existed. In both schools every endeavour was being made through booklets, leaflets and policy documents to widen the school community's knowledge of where staff responsibilities lie.

Boundary management

Every restructuring school, at whatever stage of development, must consider which aspects of extension work are most applicable to its needs, and senior management must assess their current ability to command the resources to meet those needs. Boundary management is therefore not only about who does what but also about prioritising what the school can do beyond that which is demanded of it by statute. Thus, in West Town Lane, the annual summer playschool and, in Kates Hill, the language work with Asian mothers are examples of initiatives which extend the boundary into the community. If the boundary is not managed effectively, conflicts can arise between the core work of the school and its extramural activities.

Boundary management, both within and without the school, is generally more complex in secondary schools than in primary schools. The range of job specifications is wider and extra-school contacts are more numerous. It follows that, however precise job specifications may be, there are always many activities which cross the boundaries and call for *ad hoc* management decisions.

At Risca Comprehensive School there was a serious absence of boundary management before the appointment of the present incumbent. Staff who had then been in post commented on the lack of communication and of clearly devolved responsibility and centralised decision making as features of the previous regime which made it difficult for them to understand where boundaries were to be drawn. This has now changed and staff are appreciative of the clarity of the present in-school construct.

Other concerns for boundary management relate largely to the considerable amount of available space in the school; built for 1,000 pupils, its pupil numbers had dropped to little more than 600, though they are now increasing. There seems to be little threat of school closure, for geographical reasons, though there are two accessible schools for parents who want to exercise a choice. The situation is not without its problems: relationships with the other two secondary schools must be maintained, yet at the same time those with the two primary schools must be strengthened so that parents see for themselves the advantage of continuity to the local secondary school.

Peers School is a community school with a considerable reputation for outreach and has established with many external organisations an unobtrusive boundary management. Since the school seems not to be in any way proprietorial of its physical and curricular boundaries, this style of management is largely taken for granted.

Relationships

Interpersonal relationships in any organisation wholly or largely dependent on people are vital to its success. Not surprisingly, therefore, relationships are a key feature of the restructuring school.

Staff relationships

Good staff relationships depend to a great extent on communication, both vertical and lateral. In any institution as dependent as a school on the goodwill of its staff for its development and achievement, failure to communicate will inevitably inhibit relationships. Some schools excuse their failures to communicate on the grounds that there is not the time. There is, however, a greater cost in not communicating, not merely in the time it takes to remedy such omissions but also in the weakening of trust.

In all five schools there is ample evidence, both in the details of the schools' management procedures and from the interview data, of structures which ensure good communication and consequently contribute to good staff relationships. Outside the structures are the informal relationships that the researcher observed in the staffroom, around the school and after school.

That good staff relationships derive from the example set by the headteacher is a truism. All five headteachers set the tone by their accessibility to staff and responsiveness to staff concerns. At the same time, staff understand that more complex issues cannot be solved in a corridor, or a corner of the classroom or staffroom. The ability to distinguish between levels of urgency is an important aspect both of staff development and of school management.

The decision by the headteachers of the three primary schools to create time for coordinators to visit classes was a further promotion of mutually supportive staff relationships, since it brought teachers together in a developing professional relationship. For Kates Hill, this strategy was imperative since self-monitoring procedures routinely require these opportunities (Rhoden 1997). In Risca the paired classrooms, and therefore the opportunities for shared teaching, promote a corporate professionalism. In all three schools the headteachers' commitment routinely to spend time in classrooms is a powerful agent in breaking down barriers.

The extent of staff relationships in all three schools is observable in the partnership between teaching and ancillary staff, and particularly in the message given by the display of staff photographs in the foyer of the three primary schools in which secretaries, National Nursery Education Board and general assistants, dinner ladies and caretakers appear alongside teachers.

A feature of all the schools is the non-hierarchical mutual relationship of staff. The management teams had done much to set the tone for this, being highly visible: around the school, in the staffroom, at the lunch tables. They practise an open-door policy which does much to encourage other staff to be no less approachable.

Staff development

All five schools have precise staff development policies, differing only slightly from school to school. In West Town Lane, for example, the annual allocation from the school budget for staff development is made by the management team, and the term-to-term detail is the responsibility of the headteacher.

All five schools had their own means of determining staff development needs. All use appraisal as one key factor in this determination but, particularly in Risca Comprehensive School, where appraisal was previously unknown, staff also contributed their view of their individual needs in less formal one-to-one sessions with the headteacher to ensure that they had a stake in their own development.

In all five schools INSET days and staff meetings played a significant part in staff development. While external agencies may have a contribution to make, these schools see staff development as largely an internal matter. Their common policy can be summed up as ensuring that staff

- are informed about the way in which decisions on staff development are made;
- know the amount of money available;
- have access to the headteacher or a named senior member of staff to discuss their needs as they see them;

and that governors

- are kept informed about staff development needs and the extent to which they are being met within the budget allocation.

Parental involvement

Each of the three primary schools encountered initial difficulties over the involvement of parents in the school. For all three there was no previous tradition of parental involvement; indeed the previous headteachers had not encouraged parents to concern themselves with school affairs. Parents' evenings, if they happened, were merely perfunctory.

The changes brought about in these schools, in two of the three in a very short time, are noteworthy. Parents' evenings are now social occasions as well as the opportunity for a detailed discussion of the children's progress with the class teacher. Kates Hill, with its large Asian population, has broken through the language barrier by using translators where necessary. All the headteachers had an open-door policy.

In all three primary schools the involvement of parents was being achieved by the promotion of teacher–family partnerships. At Kates Hill, considerable efforts have been made to bridge language barriers by a variety of measures: among them the use of community languages on all school signs, letters to parents in their own first language, basic English classes for Asian mothers, the welcoming of older siblings, usually ex-pupils, as translators at face-to-face parents' evenings. The welcoming of parents into the school for class assemblies, often followed by a coffee morning, has been an important icebreaker, and the summer playschool at West Town Lane and the

Christmas play at Risca were considered by staff as turning points in staff–parent relations. In West Town Lane, in particular, staff have found it easy to assemble parents' workshops for making resources: for example, puppets for the Oxford Reading Scheme, making and laminating reading and language games.

Much was learnt simply by observing parents, usually mothers, bringing their children to school and collecting them at the end of the day. Parental involvement was less easy to observe in secondary schools. Its main manifestation is in the way parents come to discuss the progress and the wellbeing of their sons and daughters. For Risca Comprehensive School parents this was a recent development, and there was clearly some hesitancy still, despite the published school policy and the obvious encouragement given by staff. In spite of these efforts, the response of parents to key issues such as pupil attendance was disappointing – unauthorised absence for the school year 1994–95 was an unacceptable 23 per cent. Some parents had helped in the organisation of the new library and it was planned that further working parties will be established as opportunities arise.

At Peers School these relationships had been built up over a far longer period, and were consolidated by the fact that so many parents are encountered informally in the community and through their use of campus facilities such as the library. The school was pro-active in contacting individual parents at the first sign of any difficulty, academic or social. The role of the school counsellor, in support of the tutors, is invaluable here.

Community perceptions

West Town Lane is geographically remote from any community other than that of the residential area in which the school is sited. It does, however, have a good record for charitable concerns, and its links with a Romanian primary school have come about through the visit there of a young member of staff. This link is not merely charitable, but includes the exchange of information through class letters that enables the pupils in both schools to gain a greater understanding of the conditions in which their peers live and work. The nature trail that the school set up in its grounds is a valuable means of informing the community about environmental concerns. Parents and members of the community helped both in the planning and in the physical work involved.

Risca Primary School has the advantage of being well placed geographically within its community, and of having a community that is increasingly prepared to take to its heart its new school. The attitude of the school initially took people by surprise: evenings for the community as well as parents to see the new building and its facilities were an early indication of the school's openness.

Kates Hill was even more closely identified with its community; Dudley, like many West Midland towns, is an aggregation of small village-like communities. There are shops down the road from the school and small-scale industries abound. Since many of these are run by members of the Asian community, news about the school spreads rapidly through the mosques, temples and *gurdwaras*. The headteacher makes a point of inviting the local religious leaders of all faiths and denominations to visit the school, and she and other staff visit places of worship at times of religious festivals.

When it won a Jerwood Award of £500 the school was able to set up in a spare mobile classroom a small community room initially for the mothers of children in the nursery. To begin with it was used by a disproportionate number of white parents, but gradually the balance has shifted so that now more Asian mothers come. It has a social function, but also provides a venue where parents can help in making resources for the school, and thus attracts fathers as well as mothers.

The availability of space at Risca Comprehensive School has prompted the headteacher's determination that there should be greater community use of the school as a means of encouraging a sense of ownership. Community groups already have physical links with the school through the on-site, but independently managed, sports and leisure complex. Developing greater cohesion between the school and these facilities is, however, a matter of some delicacy, as in the past there has been little or no contact. The headteacher's previous experience in community education may well prove to be the bridge whereby joint use can be established, but this in itself will call for highly skilled management of a kind for which there is no local precedent and minimal LEA precedent.

Peers is a recognised community school. The inclusion on the campus of a multiplicity of community organisations and one major centre of employment has taken place over a number of years. It is likely that the gradual additions of these facilities had led to the acceptance by any new users of standards and relationships built up over a period of time. The managerial openness of the school leadership and the involvement of staff in such a multiplicity of ventures seem to have resulted in an understood rather than an overt collaborative management of the community activities that take place within and without the campus. The most recent venture, the Peers Early Education Project, is an interesting indication of the school's long-term view of the way such community action will eventually lead to higher standards of achievement by its pupils, though the basic reason for its promotion of and support for the scheme is undoubtedly more altruistic than that.

Governor responsibilities

Risca Primary School and West Town Lane have effective mechanisms in place for keeping governors informed of curricular developments. Each governor at these schools undertakes responsibility for the monitoring of a particular curriculum area. When curricular issues arise at meetings of the governing body there is at least one governor who has up-to-date knowledge of what is happening in each subject area. At Kates Hill the lack of governor availability during the day has made it less easy to adopt this policy, but the headteacher takes the opportunity at each governors' meeting of having a member of staff present to speak to and be questioned on one aspect of the curriculum. The recent increase in the number of Asian and Afro-Caribbean governors reflects the efforts made to encourage representation from these communities in the affairs of the school.

That all five governing bodies have now adopted a committee structure with delegated responsibilities has relieved some of the pressures on what is a demanding appointment. Delegation has its benefits for the school as well as the governors, since headteachers know to which governor or group of governors to turn in any particular situation. Nevertheless, at Risca Comprehensive School the headteacher and the senior staff responsible for the year groups have encountered some difficulties over the management of the boundaries between governor and school responsibilities. The governors of this school have apparently not as yet come to terms with their responsibilities under local management. The headteacher is seeking to remedy this, in part, by a one-day workshop specifically for governors and senior staff and, in part, by promoting the greater involvement of governors with the school and the staff in general. The timing of this venture is important. By mid-October 1996 half the LEA and coopted members of the governing body had reached the end of their term of office and, with new appointments being made, it was opportune to encourage all to extend their understanding of their role.

Peers School is fortunate in its governing body. The family continuity in chairmanship from father to son over so long a period is a rarity, and conveys a message to other governors that dedication to the school is not achieved through token appearances at school functions and by short-term stints of service. Parent and staff governors appear to have equal status on the governing body as of right. In some schools these governors are excluded from key committees, on the grounds that they are interested parties. This was not the intention of the Education (No. 2) Act (DES 1986b).

A former teacher in the school, now its bursar, is clerk to the governing body. It was clear in discussion with him that his role as servant to the governors was important, far more so than that of many LEA officials in the past, whose main functions were to take minutes and to undertake to supply answers to governors' questions. The bursar's knowledge of the school's finances is particularly valuable to meetings of the finance committee, and the staff of the school rely on him to achieve the best results within the limits of the school budget.

Rules

In my training and consultancy work on restructuring I have encountered some resistance to this heading. Corbett might have used a more appropriate word, since his concept of 'rules' has not the rigidity of what is and what is not permitted, but relates rather to

> the behaviors and beliefs that embody the values and beliefs that professional educators and parents hold about schooling. . . . The most important rules relative to the issue of restructuring are those embedded in the vision of what 'ought to be.' Vision supplies purpose and direction.
>
> (Corbett 1990: 3)

It is usual these days to encapsulate 'vision' in the school's mission statement. Cynics have been known to remark that anyone can create a mission statement on the back of a used envelope in a few minutes. Yet in any school which regards the mission statement as an important pledge of the values it believes in, the wording of the statement is given prominence in the published policies and is revisited to ensure that it has not become a mere form of words. OFSTED inspectors are required to look for 'a positive ethos which reflects the school's commitment to high achievement, an effective learning environment, good relationships and equality of opportunity for all pupils' (OFSTED 1993: 100). A school's ethos derives from its vision as expressed in its mission statement. Each of the five schools presents its mission statement in marginally different forms and words, but nevertheless meets both the central expectation of Corbett and the criteria of the OFSTED inspectorate.

School policies

In all five schools policies are well presented, written in jargon-free language, approved by governors, readily available to parents and others and, above all, routinely revisited. Schools set up a schedule for the creation of the original set of school policies, encouraged coordinators to use staff teams to write the curriculum policies, and established a house style for presentation and content. More general policies, on pupil behaviour for example, were the work of the management team and these, as well as the curriculum documents, were overseen for final approval by the headteacher. A review programme ensures that policies continue to reflect, and be reflected in, practice.

In Kates Hill the introduction of quality control required a further review of the way policies were written so that they met the criteria of BS 5750. Similarly, the annual audit promoted the need for continual updating of policy documents. When the school went a stage further in its management development and set up the machinery whereby it could become a self-monitoring school (White and Poster 1997), drafts of school policies were shared with staff, modified and agreed.

The schools set out their policies in the year prospectus. Risca Comprehensive School, for example, gives parents and others interested an outline of what the school stands for. It begins with aims, as might be expected, and each section that follows relates to these aims: the curriculum, the pastoral organisation, enrichment and sporting activities, careers education and work experience. The section on links with parents exemplifies the school's determination to establish a partnership contract in which both what the school undertakes to do and what the school expects of cooperative parents are clearly set down. Examination results are also included in full. Such openness in the school policy documentation had previously been lacking.

Peers School presents its policies in a series of colour-coded one-sheet brochures, folded in three. They are eminently readable and the presentation allows for a revision whenever it may be necessary, rather than requiring the republishing of an entire policy document.

Financial control

The annual decline in the amount of money allocated to school budgets has been a major concern for all schools, but for the primary schools in particular. Each headteacher has been adamant that staffing and class size must be maintained wherever possible. All staff are informed and involved, particularly where decisions have to be made within a limited time. That any of the primary schools would achieve much by going to the parents or the community for support, financial or in kind, is unlikely: Kates Hill is in an area of high unemployment; Risca Primary is a new school but may well be developing a tradition of community support, as shown by the voluntary professional contribution to the design and preparation of its school.

In both secondary schools there are excellent control systems. The headteacher of Risca Comprehensive School has turned a deficit budget in January 1994 to one which now enables new developments, such as the employment of a library technician, to be initiated after staffing and material demands have been met. She has established a clear procedure whereby the management team receives budget requests, considers them in the light of the total money available, and informs staff personally whenever a request cannot be met in full. It is then the responsibility of the departmental or other sub-budget holder to ensure that there is no overspending. This has led to a realistic approach by staff to matching needs with the availability of funds. A great sense of relief that they are no longer subject to the whim of one person for the distribution of resources was evident in several of the staff interviews.

Peers School has, as a community school, a far more complex budget, one that would be difficult to control were it not for the appointment of the bursar. His role as clerk to the governors has already been referred to, and his service to the finance committee is invaluable. Decisions on the provision of departmental and other funds are, of course, made by the management team, in full consultation with sub-budget holders, but the bursar is able to give up-to-date information on expenditure and balances.

The contribution of governors to financial control in the two secondary schools could not be more different. At Risca Comprehensive, the finance committee has on a number of occasions been inquorate, and the headteacher has had, illegally, she believes, to take sole responsibility for financial decisions. It is to be hoped that new appointments have strengthened the committee so that it now meets its responsibilities under the Act. The Peers governors, in contrast, play a considerable role in financial decision making and in seeking funding from sources other than the LEA budget for a wide range of activities.

Administration systems

All five headteachers had set up clear-cut and easily manageable systems. The interview of the West Town Lane School secretary gave evidence of the importance of providing office staff with a wide remit. Her statement that, in a small school where the headteacher is by no means 'office-bound', she has to deal with many immediate situations is borne out by observations made in the other two primary schools. Because situations cannot always be foreseen, no headteacher can define precise rules for a secretary's role and responsibilities; the closeness of their relationship in these schools establishes the boundaries by common sense and, sometimes, by trial and error.

The office administration in the secondary schools was no less efficient. With an older age range, both schools use a rota of pupils at a table in front of the school office to be the first point of contact for visitors. Where necessary, after visitors have stated their business to the office staff, the pupils will guide them to their destination or take them on a tour of the school. Peers School has a wide range of visitors – as the signing-in sheet stating purpose of visit and times of arrival and departure demonstrates – and issues clip-on badges so that those going around the school can be recognised as bona fide visitors. Anyone wishing to see the headteacher, deputy heads or, as at Risca Comprehensive, the school nurse, each of whom has a room behind the secretaries' office, is escorted by a secretary and shown to a pleasant waiting area where there are magazines and school brochures. In each school I was greeted by my host almost before I had time to sit down, and his observation was that this was the general practice save when the secretary had already apologised that the host would still be engaged for a short time or was elsewhere in the school building.

Secretarial staff in all the schools had clear job descriptions, though in the larger secondary schools the reception of visitors appeared to be the responsibility of whichever secretary was available. Staff were satisfied with the degree of support, for typing and replication for example, that they received, though there was also much self-help. It was evident in both secondary schools that technicians were freeing faculty staff as far as possible from much responsibility for routine administration.

It is not only in the school office that administration systems obtain. Teaching staff need clear guidelines over their role and responsibilities in matters such as pupil absences, dealing with aberrant behaviour, fire and safety regulations, accident procedures, record-keeping and the like. All five schools have well-presented staff handbooks that cover these areas and, importantly, a policy for updating these documents regularly.

Each secondary school has a member of staff designated as examinations officer, with responsibility in Peers School for a wide range of examinations in GCSE, A level, GNVQ and other external qualifications. The range in an 11–16 school is not so extensive, but still demanding, and growing as the school embarks on GNVQ options in Years 10 and 11.

The status of office, caretaking, cleaning and school-meals staff is high and the standard of pupil behaviour – courtesy to ancillary staff, the absence of litter and graffiti, for example – endorses the concern of all five schools that these are members of staff no less than those working in the classrooms.

Results

School development plan review

Thomas and Martin (1996: 34–5) cite a survey of 800 schools, 95 per cent of which had development plans. The authors identify four stages in the conventional cycle of development planning:

1 the need for audit in order to review the school's current strengths and weaknesses in relation to its aims;
2 the identification of priorities which will allow the school to close the gap between its current position and its intended objectives;
3 deciding upon the best means for implementing proposed changes;
4 ensuring that progress is being reliably implemented.

The relationship between development plan, monitoring and evaluation, and quality control is clearly established.

In all five schools the development plan is the basis of current and future year activities. All adopt at least a three-year cycle, in which review takes place annually: to provide an evaluation of the year now ending, to consolidate, to add to or modify in the light of experience the plan for the coming year, and to develop in greater detail those for subsequent years. There is ample documentary evidence that this is no paper exercise, but one involving the participation of all staff and the governing body.

For Risca Comprehensive School, the appointment in 1994 of the new headteacher saw the first development plan the school had known. The 1994–95 plan is a compendious document, setting out in a wide range of pastoral and curricular areas priorities, targets, success criteria, action plans with dates for completion, and a programme of interim and end-of-stage reviews.

The success of the first plan can best be judged from the review which is contained in the 1995–96 plan. The school was able now to shift the focus from curriculum development and the establishment of a pastoral system to whole-school issues. No less important was the ability of the management team to create and promote charts showing a four-year plan under the headings of curriculum, school organisation and building development. The first year of the four-year plan was in fact a review of 1994–95, to ensure that achievement was both assessed and recognised and that in every case the proposed continuity over the next three years was clearly indicated.

Monitoring and evaluation

One of the three primary schools, Kates Hill, has set up a detailed system of monitoring and evaluation that evolved initially from the perception of the audit needs implicit in its involvement in BS 5750. The rationale for and the practical details of the system are explained in the book *The Self-Monitoring School* (White and Poster 1997).

Risca Primary was inspected by an OFSTED team in June 1996. External evaluation by experienced inspectors may be advantageous, not least for a new school, but it is important to recognise, as some inspections do not, that restructuring is a lengthy and ongoing process. The snapshot approach of an external inspection may not give a fair picture of a school's development. The headteacher of Risca Primary is, however, clear that her own evaluation procedures have benefited from preparation for the external inspection.

There was no formal system for monitoring and evaluation at West Town Lane. The headteacher believes that her regular overseeing of all six classes, and particularly the fact that she herself engages routinely in teaching at all levels in tandem with the class teacher, give her a good understanding of the teaching and learning standards and processes. She required all staff, however experienced, to discuss with her their lesson plans and to review the outcomes routinely. Evaluation of the outcomes of particular aspects of the National Curriculum occurs frequently between the teachers of the parallel year groups, and staff are developing self-monitoring procedures, though as yet without the formal structures to be found in Kates Hill.

There is ample evidence from the Risca Comprehensive School documentation that monitoring has featured prominently in the transition from the one-year (1994–95) plan to the three-year rolling programme that succeeded it. However, monitoring at this level was largely in the hands of the headteacher and management team. Proposals for more decentralised monitoring evolved in the curriculum development plans for 1995–96, prepared by heads of faculty, in all of which termly reviews feature. An expressed need in some plans for training in monitoring and evaluation of the curriculum was met by a staff in-service training day so that there is now common ground in the methodology used and the way the findings are translated into action. One faculty considers as an aspect of monitoring, in addition to the curriculum content and delivery, the effectiveness in terms of pupil achievement, and is conducting a longitudinal study of a sample of pupils to seek answers to the questions: do pupils know how to improve; and as a result, are they improving?

When the faculties are confident that they have established sound curricula to meet the needs of all pupils and effective teamworking to cover a multiplicity of demands on staff time, there will be the opportunity for whole-school monitoring and evaluation.

Pupil performance

That there were significant differences in the performance standards reached in the three primary schools is obvious from the statistics of SATs at Key Stage 1 for all three schools and Key Stage 2 for the two full-range primary schools. From performance results it can be seen that West Town Lane, the school in the socially most advantaged area, was the best achiever. Yet all three primary schools are far more interested in year-on-year progress in pupil performance.

Both secondary schools are, like many others, diversifying the curriculum to introduce examinations other than GCSE. There has been no recognition yet from the DfEE that this will have any effect on the statistics of A–C GCSE results.

Quality control

Only in Kates Hill is there evidence of a systematic approach to quality control, in that case through BS 5750. Both Kates Hill and Risca Primary have certification through Investors in People (IIP), the triennial review element of which is to some extent a measure of quality.

It is, however, a mistake to assume that a school that has not adopted any of the recognised procedures has no interest in quality control. The annual audit of the school development plan evident in the documentation of the other three schools may well provide sufficient information for some form of quality control.

Summary

An analysis of these schools using the framework in Table 10.1 indicates that all five schools are, having due regard to the length of time the present headteachers have been in post and to local circumstances, already effective schools in most areas of activity. Where there are weaknesses, these are recognised, and their remediation is considered in the school development plans. At a time when the morale of teachers in so many schools is at a low ebb, the enthusiasm of all staff in these schools is encouraging and a reflection of the support of peers and the leadership at all levels.

These schools may reasonably be judged to have met the criteria of the restructuring school, though all appear to have a clear understanding that constant vigilance is required to maintain the standards they have set for themselves. There is no such thing as *stasis* in restructuring schools.

11

RESTRUCTURING: CONCLUSIONS FROM THE CASE STUDIES

Introduction

The final chapter sets out to answer a number of key questions that have arisen from the case studies in Chapters 5–9 and the analysis in Chapter 10:

- Are the case study schools, selected because they gave promise of meeting the restructuring criteria, in any way radically different from other effective schools?
- Is restructuring compatible with centralised decision making?
- Are school governing bodies sufficiently cognisant of their role to understand and promote restructuring processes?
- Can inspection be a significant change agent in restructuring? Are there other change agents that might be called upon to promote restructuring processes in schools?
- What pitfalls to the restructuring process have been identified, either in the literature on the topic or in the case studies?
- Given the dearth of educational literature relevant to restructuring in England and Wales, how likely is it that those in our schools will be able to make the transition, as it has been described in transatlantic and antipodean case studies and conditions?
- Will new structures stay restructured?

The distinctive features of the restructuring school

The research evidence, assessed in Chapter 10, would appear to indicate that there are recognisable features of the restructuring school that may or may not be present in effective schools. Restructuring demands a holistic approach and therefore a constant re-examination of the school's policies, processes and practice. The effective school may be effective in its current state, but there is no guarantee, without the underpinning of a holistic approach, that it will respond successfully to internal or external change factors. There must be a structure for managing organic development which is both strong enough and elastic enough to meet innovation needs without sacrificing essential stability. Furthermore, Cuban (1988: 342) argues that 'first-order change', which tries to improve on what exists without significant or substantial change, is not effective; 'second-order change' that restructures the school into new ways which will solve problems is essential. There are five elements which are crucial to restructuring.

1   The restructuring school has *vision*. '[This] is a trite term . . . and at various times it refers to mission, purpose, goals, objectives or a sheet of paper posted near the principal's office', wrote Isaacson and Bamburg (1992: 42). It is easy to construct a mission statement of all that is desirable for a school to aim to achieve, but more difficult to supply the means whereby it may be implemented. Dunham (1995: 121) quotes the acting headteacher of a secondary school concerned about school improvement in his institution: 'We need a restatement of the vision for the future of the school and a long-term plan to realise that vision. . . . This can only be accomplished within an informed context and over a clear time span.'

2   The phrase 'within an informed context and over a clear time span' points to the second key element in the restructuring school: the existence of a school development *plan* which derives from a rigorous examination of the present situation, is specific in its objectives, applies to them, as far as possible, timetables for progressive future achievement and sets up a programme of monitoring and evaluation. The plan is not, as it would seem to be in some schools, an end in itself: the writing of it will never automatically lead to its effective implementation. That can only happen when the plan is integrated with an overt statement, known to all staff and agreed by them, of how and with what priority its elements will be achieved, and at what stages and by what processes it will be monitored and evaluated. For restructuring plans to be modified or certain elements postponed is not necessarily an admission of failure, but rather a response to the reality of changing priorities. Nevertheless, modifications to a development plan should be undertaken only after careful consideration of their impact on the plan as a whole, and care should be taken that those members of staff who have invested time and energy in preparation should not feel that their work is in vain. In a holistic programme of change, an element may be temporarily set aside, but is most unlikely to be abandoned.

3   This, then, points to the third prerequisite of the restructuring school: a programme of *monitoring and evaluation*, the processes of which are fully understood by all staff and the outcomes of which are made known to all stakeholders – defined by Aspinwall *et al.* (1992) as 'any group or individual who is affected by or can affect the future of the organisation, programme or activity'. It follows that the restructuring school must not delude itself and others by being selective about the outcomes, publicising

those that it has achieved and finding ways of disguising its shortcomings. Equally, it must not be deluded into making comparisons of its achievements with other schools', even where this appears to be to its own advantage. One concern of evaluation is the identification of year-on-year progress, particularly but by no means exclusively in pupil learning: the so-called 'value-added element'.

4   No school will succeed in restructuring without the fourth element, *staff commitment*, which derives from a common sense of purpose found as readily in the newly qualified teacher as in the senior management team, and in ancillary staff no less than in the teaching staff. This does not come about 'on demand'. Commitment is obtained by sound communication and by the sharing of the decision-making process wherever this is possible. Darling-Hammond (1996) points out that US schools which are effective in curriculum and teacher development provide 'structured time . . . for teachers to work together on professional issues'. We know that, whatever the constraints on teacher time – 'time, or more properly lack of it, is one of the most difficult problems faced by schools' (Watts and Castle 1993: 306) – this need for structured time is equally true of schools on this side of the Atlantic. Without a high level of staff commitment allied with a corporate consensus on the prioritisation of issues, 'working together on professional issues' will not be achieved effectively. Hord (1996: 2) uses the term 'professional community of learners' for those teachers in schools whose 'goal is to enhance their effectiveness as professionals in the schools for students' benefit'. To achieve this, curriculum coordinators in primary schools, departmental and faculty heads and pastoral leaders in secondary schools, need structured time for planning and for group work with their colleagues. That it needs a commitment well beyond the 1,265 hours of the teacher's written contract is evident. It is therefore essential that, at every level, commitment is recognised and praised.

5   Finally, restructuring is achieved and maintained by sound and effective *leadership*. This is the key to a school's effectiveness. It is often believed by headteachers that leadership rests with them or with a hierarchy in which they are the controlling element. The five case studies in Chapters 5–9, and the published accounts of US research into restructuring schools, supply ample evidence that, while the leadership of the headteacher or principal is fundamental to their success, the dissemination to other staff of leadership roles is no less important. A key task of the headteacher is to ensure that the boundaries of these roles are well managed – in a way which allows for initiative but does not lead to role conflict – and that, through appraisal, staff development interviews and the evaluation of job specifications, there is a regular review of achievement and shortcomings. It might be thought that there is a distinctive leadership style relevant to the restructuring school. The case studies suggest that this is not so. One indicator of their success is that in each case a situational or contextual leadership style has

been adopted that suits the school's needs at a particular stage of restructuring.

Restructuring and centralised decision making

Caldwell and Spinks (1988) were powerful pioneers of the self-managing school. At the time of the publication of their book, they cited a wide range of decision making as 'increasingly being delegated to schools' (ibid.: 5), including knowledge, technology, power, material, people, time and finance. With the introduction in England and Wales of legislation for local financial management (LFM) and local management of schools (LMS) in the year of publication of Caldwell and Spinks' influential book, it might have been thought that the government of that period was promoting a similar decentralisation of decision making. On the contrary there has been, *de facto*, an ever-increasing central control over each of those areas.

It is necessary now to ask how far present-day constraints in these areas inhibit the development of restructuring. Certainly the case study schools appear not to have found them a serious impediment to their development plans. In each case the school leadership has assessed the present situation of the school and what changes would be needed to restructure it to become substantially more effective, and worked out a staged programme in which change can be planned, monitored and reviewed. These schools appear to have worked within the boundaries of external controls without compromising their goals or their time schemes. It is important to recognise that Conley's 'road map to restructuring' is just that; a school must determine its own route and time plan for its journey to its destination.

School governing bodies and restructuring

When Conley (1993) placed 'governance' as one of the four enabling factors for restructuring, he was underlining the continuing importance of local decision making, and not proposing any major innovation or power shift.

In England and Wales, 'the conduct of a school is under the direction of the governing body, except to the extent that the [Education No. 2, 1986] Act assigns functions to anyone else (§16.1)'. This is both a radical change to the governance of English and Welsh state schools and an awesome responsibility. Even a decade later the implications do not appear to be fully appreciated in a substantial number of schools. Governors are now required to decide what the curricular aims of the school shall be and their conclusions must be the subject of a written statement which is kept up to date (§18.2). Implicit in the latter part of this requirement is that they are familiar with the curricular aims contained in the school development plan, and, particularly, that they are informed about the results of the annual review of the plan, shortcomings no less than achievements. This is a key element in the expectation of accountability in governors, yet research evidence (e.g. Baginsky *et al*. 1991) indicates that, in half their case study schools, a draft of the school aims written by the headteacher had gone through without discussion.

Nowhere is the function of the governing body more precisely defined than in its responsibilities following an OFSTED inspection: it is charged with providing an action plan within forty days in response to points raised in the report. Within their BEMAS research project (Ouston *et al*. 1996) on school improvement through external inspection, conducted by means of surveys of schools inspected in 1994 and 1995, there is clear evidence that many governing bodies did not appreciate that they themselves, not the school staff, are responsible for the creation of the action plan. Nevertheless, in OFSTED documents it is repeatedly referred to as 'the governors' action plan' and failure to respond lies at their door. The 1994 survey 'found that almost half the respondents commented that the governing body played little or no part in its creation', and the 1995 survey 'showed evidence of [only] a little more involvement by governors' (Earley 1996). In this vital area many governing bodies, it would appear, are not fulfilling their legal responsibilities, as required of them by an agency of the DfEE. Yet in addition to these, under the 1997 Education Act, it appears that they will also be required to set targets in relation to pupil performance.

The provision of an annual report and the convening of an annual parents' meeting are precise responsibilities of the governing body under the Education Act of 1986. The first research study on the way these responsibilities were being discharged (Earley 1988) included a national overview by the NFER School Governors' Research Group. It was critical of the language used in many reports: abbreviations without explanation (for example, PTR), and jargon: 'so often the reports appeared to be written by educationalists for educationalists'.

The headteacher of Risca Primary School considered that the low standard of presentation of the annual report, while the responsibility of the governing body rather than of the headteacher, would reflect adversely on the school. She persuaded the chair of governors to convene a workshop of one representative of each governor category – parent, staff, LEA, community – to plan and prepare a section of the report. The headteacher advised on the legal requirements of the report and, with the chair, edited the final version. While the report was well received by parents, and won a national commendation, it did little to enhance the numbers attending the annual parents' meeting. That, for the headteacher and the governing body, was to be the next challenge.

If these research findings and school experiences remain an accurate representation of governors' understanding of their accountability – and there is no evidence to suggest otherwise – is it likely that they will appreciate and, even more important, support the radical changes that are taking place in restructuring schools? For the restructuring school, with its holistic approach to all aspects of management, the absence of a committed and involved governing body would be a serious handicap. The evidence from the case study schools is that there must be a policy of encouraging sustained governor involvement in the change processes in which the school is engaged. This will come only from the consistent efforts of the headteacher and the staff to promote governor understanding and activity. The best example of achievement is to be found in the West Town Lane case study (Chapter 5), but all the case study schools give this issue a high priority. If governing bodies are not actively involved in the restructuring process, the collaboration of all stakeholders towards the school's developmental goals will be severely weakened.

Change agents in restructuring

Before the emasculation of the advisory service in many LEAs as a result of increasing cuts in local authority funding, advisers were well placed to work alongside schools in promoting change. Most advisers had, and in some LEAs still have, dual functions: as subject specialists and for the servicing of a group of schools. This latter function was no less important than the former since the adviser provided a liaison service between the primary and secondary schools within a geographical area and were able to promote bridging activities in an age when most primary schools, even in urban areas, were aptly described as 'feeder schools' to a specific secondary school. The former function remains, though in most areas much curtailed and in some LEAs subject to an on-charge against the school budget. The latter function has very largely been taken over by the secondary school, and its purpose has been changed, since the introduction of parental choice, from collaboration to marketing.

There were other important aspects of the work of HMI, now no more than a footnote in history. Lawton and Gordon (1987) in a section headed 'The secondary Inspectorate and the curriculum' refer to the national survey undertaken by HMI over a three-year period ending in 1978 covering a 10 per cent sample of pupils in their fourth and fifth years of secondary education. Because HMI had 'a brief that went beyond inspection to include disseminating good practice' (Earley et al. 1996: 1), as in *Ten Good Schools* (DES 1977), *Teaching Quality* (DES 1983a), *Better Schools* (DES 1985), for example, relatively few schools were visited, and those that were, moreover, were selected because they were likely to provide data to inform national policy. The 1992 Education Act abandoned this approach and brought into being the Office for Standards in Education (OFSTED) with a remit to introduce school inspections, conducted by a team of trained inspectors and led by a registered inspector. Regardless of government enthusiasm for the scheme, what needs to be considered is:

- whether the exercise is cost-effective; and
- whether there are alternatives to external inspection that might be more effective, less costly and achieved with far less documentation, strain on the school's resources, and stress on the school staff, teachers and ancillaries alike.

The OFSTED budget for inspection is estimated at £100 million a year (Earley *et al.* 1996: 11).

The main merit of inspection claimed by OFSTED is the inspectors' identification of key issues and the requirement on the governing body to produce an action plan 'within forty working days of the publication of the inspection report' (DfEE 1993) to remedy deficiencies. It may be, however, that what OFSTED regards as deficiencies appear in the school development plan for future years; the school will usually know the rate of change that its staff, coping with a limited budget for resources, with year-on-year changes in the National Curriculum, and with a barrage of criticism, often from ill-informed sources such as the tabloid press, can sustain. Earley *et al.* (1996: 19–20) cited as one of the findings of their BEMAS research in 1995 this effect of inspection on school development:

> Some respondents explained that the process of preparing for the inspection had prevented developments they wished to make, whilst others noted it had led them to make developments earlier than they might have done.

Undoubtedly inspection by experienced and trained educators can contribute to school improvement. However, it has to be questioned whether the way to achieve effective change is through a five-day visitation once in four years, followed by a report and a requirement for the governors to produce an action plan, the implementation of which is only monitored by OFSTED in extreme cases. Sir Brian Nicholson, former president of the Confederation of British Industry, castigated OFSTED for running an inspection service which caused 'a brief frenzy in the staff room without any follow-up to establish long-term solutions. . . . It is time to restore [the LEA] role of monitoring and helping schools to deliver higher standards' (Nicholson 1997).

Research evidence in the Rand Change Agent study in the USA indicated that

> it is exceedingly difficult for policy to change practice. . . . Contrary to the one-to-one relationship assumed to exist between policy and practice . . . the nature, amount, and the pace of change at the local level was a product of local factors that were largely beyond the control of higher-level policy makers.
>
> (McLaughlin 1990: 12)

This led McLaughlin to conclude that 'policy cannot mandate what matters; implementation dominates outcomes; local variability is the rule – uniformity is the exception' (cited in Hopkins and Lagerweij 1996). A prerequisite of restructuring, as of all school improvement, is that the school both desires change and is capable of managing it. In this respect the school is therefore the primary change agent, though clearly it may need support and advice. Consultancy is one possible means to this end.

The LEA, even if its reduction in status were reversed, is not the only body that might take on a consultancy role, where this would be advantageous to the school. University departments of education, either through funded research projects or cost-based support, are possible consultants. Within their chapter 'Improving the quality of education for all', Hopkins *et al.* (1994: 109) rightly emphasise the need for a formal contract based on a set of ground rules that require 'from the outset that collaborating LEAs and project team members all demonstrate real commitment to the project'. These conditions apply, of course, to a specific research project initiated by staff of the Institute of Education, University of Cambridge, but there is no reason why they should not be applied as rigorously to a contract between any university body and any school or group of schools seeking support through a consultancy.

The National Education Assessment Centre (NEAC) provides an assessment of headteacher participants in a two-day workshop in four broad areas: administrative, interpersonal, communicative and personal breadth. This is followed by the preparation, in collaboration with an assessor, of an action plan dealing with the individual's personal development needs as well as those of the school. NEAC's work is now expanding into assessment in selection centres for new headteachers, HEADLAMP, and middle-manager assessment centres. The director emphasises that 'centre' describes a process, not a location. NEAC is a non-judgemental change agent; the only disadvantage is that the process is expensive and unlikely to be funded from school budgets.

Whatever inspection may or may not contribute to school improvement, it is obvious that it offers little to the school embarking upon or considering restructuring. Such a school needs first to have a clear understanding of where it is now. For this it may find some help in consultancy, but its best help lies in self-assessment, through monitoring and evaluation. If it lacks the skills for this, then there can be found in a wide range of management literature the means to acquire them. Next, it needs to decide its own 'roadmap to restructuring', the route it will take to holistic change. Then it needs to plan its priorities, both within the school development plan and in its longer term aims. Finally, it needs to make public its proposals, to ensure that all stakeholders are aware of them and will give them their support. This school-based strategy implies a certain level of organisational maturity, which not all schools will be able to demonstrate.

These are the schools that need the help – even, in extreme cases, the intervention – of the LEA if the latter is to be a satisfactory change agent in restructuring.

Pitfalls in restructuring

Despite the best of intentions, it is possible for a school to lose sight of the holistic approach that is an essential feature of restructuring. This may happen when external pressures, from government, from parents, even from staff, divert attention towards a particular feature of the school's performance. For example, the intention to achieve an improved performance in GCSE and A Level examinations, while in itself highly desirable, may become, if the reasoning behind the concern is not so much the improved education of all students as the desire to climb up the league-table ladder, an overriding demand on staff time to the detriment of other restructuring needs. One of the key management tasks in the restructuring school is to maintain a balance of improvement endeavours. Since it is rarely possible to advance on all fronts at the same time, the school development plan must be specific about priorities, and staff must not only be aware of what those priorities are but must also be collectively supportive of the developmental policy. Sometimes staff, including the senior management team, must hold back on aspects of restructuring deemed to be desirable in favour of those which are more immediate. This is not a rejection of holism, but rather a sensible use of resources.

Related to this potential pitfall is what Conley (1993: 316) refers to as 'the time trap':

> Successful schools . . . direct their energies toward activities that will yield changes and improvement. At the same time they acknowledge that it takes time to implement new practices, usually several years, and that during the implementation phase there may be a time when efficiency and performance actually decrease.

Fullan and Miles (1992) refer to this as the implementation dip. There are several possible consequences of this phase, all well known to innovative schools. Teachers involved in curricular developments, often those with subordinate roles, may return to their former practices whenever difficulties arise. Highly motivated innovation leaders may invest so much of their energies in making the innovation effective that they lose sight of the importance of other long-standing commitments to school developments. Occasionally there is a loss of a sense of balance, so that pupil performance actually suffers as the support for the innovation becomes fragmented. Headteachers and senior management teams may also bear some responsibility for the implementation dip, often unwittingly in their determination to promote new ways of working, by miscalculating 'the amount of time and energy needed to achieve meaningful and sustained change, and the amount of resistance such a process engenders' (Conley 1993: 318).

A further pitfall is 'change for the sake of change'. Just as in the 1970s there were schools that too readily and without adequate preparation engaged in curriculum innovation, often because it enhanced their status as innovators, so too is it possible for schools today to seize upon restructuring as a panacea. This attitude to restructuring is more likely to add to the school's ills than to relieve them. Restructuring must be introduced within a context of understanding and support, by governors, parents, the community and the staff. It is less important that the term 'restructuring' is used and understood – indeed, it is a term still with a wide range of meanings, even within educational circles – than that there should be a broad understanding of the purpose of each aspect of development and a recognition that it accords with the school's vision as expressed in the mission statement.

Finally, 'as more and more people . . . acknowledge that the current system is not working' (David 1990: 209), there will be increasing pressure for restructuring. David continues:

> The very phrase 'structural change' signals a conception of education reform that is very different from reforms of the past. Unlike either top-down, externally imposed reforms or bottom-up, school-based improvement efforts, restructuring connotes systemic change. It grows out of a combination of
> * research findings on how people and organisations change and
> * the increasing gap between what schools look like now and what they must look like in the future to meet society's needs.
> (David 1990: 209)

The lack of knowledge about restructuring

There is, it must be said, a dearth of education management books published on this side of the Atlantic that even acknowledge the existence of restructuring. Even when titles that appear relevant can be found, there is no certainty, in advance of reading the book, of understanding the true meaning of 'restructuring' as defined by UK authors. At times one despairs on finding that restructuring can have so many meanings. Of the fourteen contributors to the best of recent books, *Restructuring and Quality: Issues for Tomorrow's Schools* (Townsend 1997), only four are working in English universities researching into aspects of restructuring. Valuable as their contributions may be, in no case is there any direct application to school restructuring. It is therefore little wonder that those in universities and schools who wish to look to the practice of restructuring as a means of enhancing school improvement and effectiveness have to turn to writers almost exclusively in North America, Australia and New Zealand; and this requires their readers to recontextualise what they read to the conditions, often significantly different, as this thesis has sought to demonstrate, under which schools operate on this side of the globe.

Will new structures stay restructured?

In the USA school restructuring has given rise to 'a great deal of well-intentioned effort, at levels varying from teaching/learning processes through to the organisation of schools, to governance systems, school-based management and parental choice' (Miles and Ekholm 1991: 63). Is there any guarantee that, once introduced, these structures will stay in place?

In the first place, there is a serious doubt among US researchers as to whether many of those who have been involved in restructuring have a clear conceptual grasp of the levels and content required (Elmore *et al.* 1990). Second, in England and Wales, so-called restructuring has been piecemeal. It has been brought about in some schools, generally perforce, by the introduction through the Education Act of 1988 of three significant areas of change: in the control of the budget (LFM), in governance (LMS) and in responsibility for the public communication of National Curriculum Key Stage results, public examination results and OFSTED inspection outcomes. Yet these changes rarely seem to have promoted a reconsideration of the organisation of the internal management of the school to meet the new situation. Innovations emanating from government have been, and still are, led by political dogma, with little regard for whether or not schools have had the time or the opportunity to develop strategic planning for change. Indeed, the internal organisation of many schools has been largely untouched by this rapid and radical change, even though it is clearly the focal point for restructuring. Change, to be effective and lasting, must be holistic.

There are clear indicators that institutionalisation is only complete when:

- change and the resources needed for it have become routine in the system;
- those involved at all levels of the change process, and not merely those who have been promoting it, accept and implement the change;
- staff, teachers and ancillaries alike, who are new to the school, are inducted into the vision as well as the operational procedures that have now become appropriate to the school.

There is, however, a common misconception about institutionalisation: that there is a purely linear relationship between innovation, implementation and institutionalisation. There is an inherent danger in this view. Unless it is recognised that the innovation is to be embedded into the system, and that steps to that end must be considered, planned and as far as possible implemented from the outset, there will always be an unexpressed but nevertheless highly significant view that 'maybe the innovation will blow itself out or simply fade away'. Of course, the ongoing monitoring and evaluation of an innovation may lead to a considered judgement that it is, after all, inappropriate to the school's mission statement or aims; in that case there may well be a decision to abandon it.

While the International School Improvement Project (see pp. 21–2) concentrated on analysis of the quality of learning, management, school leadership, teacher training, governmental and local support, inevitably there were also indicators of the processes that would lead to the ability of schools to manage change. Among these, perhaps the most significant was the identification (Miles *et al.* 1987: 83–4) of a number of key factors leading to the institutionalisation of innovation, crucial to an understanding both of what has gone wrong in so much of centrally imposed change and of the preconditions for success, either in remedial action or of innovation when schools take the initiative, as they must, in making change work.

- Innovations which are substantial, of high quality, central to organisational purposes, and reasonably well-fitting to the local setting are more likely to become institutionalised.
- Institutionalisation of a change is more likely when a school is innovative, receptive, and supports collaboration among professionals; when its structures and procedures are well-integrated, with enough human and financial resources to manage change; when there is a felt need and pressure exerted by an advocate for change.
- The external context . . . should be reasonably stable, and exerting pressure for the innovation. . . .
- The change process [demands] stable, skilled leadership, having a clear vision, and using good coordination mechanisms; active interaction and participation by users of the innovation; vigorous mobilisation and reinforcement through administrative and peer support, careful following of the innovation's progress and adaptation of it, and development of ownership through widespread, rewarding use; strong, sustained technical assistance; and direct effort to stabilise the innovation [by] widespread, good quality implementation, removing the old while embedding the new, and allocating routine resources to support the change permanently.

(Miles and Ekholm 1991)

These preconditions may seem idealistic to teachers and administrators seeking to effect change with limited human and material resources. Nevertheless, they need to be set out in such detail and with such precision, so that judgements may be made on what more might be achieved towards restructuring in schools were their resources enhanced.

There is one final point to be made in this section: for a structure to 'stay' restructured, the effective school must be prepared, as the need or opportunity arises, to develop further policies and processes in order to remain effective. While change for the sake of change is not to be encouraged in the restructuring school, *stasis* may lead to complacency, and complacency is not a good bedfellow for effectiveness.

Endpiece

It is perhaps only right that the last word should be from the one head-teacher who was, before the case study interviews, already familiar with the processes and practice of restructuring. Asked if that understanding had made any difference to the way she promoted greater effectiveness in the running of her school, she replied:

> I believe that I had early on in my headship an implicit under-standing of the importance of being specific about roles, rules, relationships and results, though I would not have used Corbett's vocabulary; but now I have an explicit understanding of their inter-connectedness.
>
> Whenever we are considering a new development to make the school more effective, we now look carefully at the way it will fit in with existing change processes. If, for example, the resources are not there, or the staff or governing body is not convinced of the merits of the proposal, then this is not the time to introduce it. It is back to the drawing board or, sometimes, putting a develop-ment on the back burner until the conditions are more favourable.
>
> There are two vital conditions for effective change: that we carry everyone with us, and that we are working to a long-term plan in which the parts make up the whole. This is what I understand by holism in restructuring.

BIBLIOGRAPHY

ACAS (1986) 'The report of the Appraisal Training Working Group', reprinted in HMSO (1989).

Adair, J. (1983) *Effective Leadership*, London: Pan.

Allen, B. (ed.) (1968) *Headship in the 1970s*, Oxford: Blackwell.

Anderson, J. (1993) 'Washington State's schools for the twenty-first century: school restructuring', paper presented at the September *1993 Conference of the International Movement towards Educational Change (IMTEC)*, Bogensee, Germany.

Anderson, M. (1993) in Ribbins, P. (1997).

Argyris, C. (1982) *Reasoning, Learning and Action: Individual and Organisation*, London: Jossey-Bass.

Argyris, C. and Schon, D. (1978) *Organisational Learning: a Theory of Action Perspective*, Reading, MA: Addison-Wesley.

Aspinwall, K., Simkins, T., Wilkinson, J. F. and McAuley, J. (eds) (1992) *Managing Evaluation in Education: a Developmental Approach*, London: Routledge.

Baginsky, M., Baker, L. and Cleave, S. (1991) *Towards Effective Partnerships in School Governance*, Slough: NFER.

Barker, H. (1993) 'The national standard of "Investor in People" – does it have a place in the management of schools?', in Green (ed.) (1993).

Baron, G. (1968) 'An overview', in Allen (ed.) (1968).

Baron, G. and Howell, D. (1974) *The Management and Government of Schools*, London: Athlone Press.

Barth, R. (1990) *Improving Schools from Within*, San Francisco: Jossey-Bass.

Bastiani, J. (1993) 'Parents and schools', in Munn (ed.) (1993).

Beare, H. and Slaughter, R. (1993) *Education for the Twenty-First Century*, London: Routledge.

Belbin, R. M. (1981) *Management Teams: Why They Succeed or Fail*, London: Heinemann.

Bell, L. and Rhodes, C. (1996) *The Skills of Primary School Management*, London: Routledge.

Beloe Report (1963), London: HMSO.

Benn, C. and Simon, B. (1972) *Half Way There*, London: McGraw-Hill.

Betts, C. (1992) *Internal Quality Audit Training*, London: British Standards Institution.

Blandford, S. (1997) *Middle Management in Schools: How to Harmonise Managing and Teaching for an Effective School*, London: Pitman.

Bollen, R. (1989) *School Improvement: a Dutch Case in International Perspective*, Leuven, Belgium: Acco.

Bollen, R. (ed.) (1993) *Educational Change Facilitators: Craftsmanship and Effectiveness*, Utrecht, Netherlands: National Centre for School Improvement.

Bolman, L. G. and Deal, T. E. (1991*) Reframing Organisations: Artistry, Choice and Leadership*, San Francisco, CA: Jossey-Bass.

Budde, R. (1989) 'Education by charter', *Phi Delta Kappan* 70(7).

Bunnell, S. and Stephens, E. (1984) 'Teacher appraisal: a democratic approach', *School Organisation* 4(4).

Burns, J. M. (1978) *Leadership*, New York: Harper.

Burns, T. and Stalker, G. M. (1968) *The Management of Innovation*, London: Tavistock.

Bush, T. *et al.* (eds.) (1980) *Approaches to School Management*, London: Harper & Row.

Caldwell, B. J. and Spinks, J. M. (1988) *The Self-managing School*, Lewes: Falmer.

Cannell, C. F. and Kahn, R. L. (1968) 'Interviewing', in G. Lindzey and A. Aronson (eds) (1968) *The Handbook of Sociol Psychology*, vol. 2: *Research Methods*, New York: Addison-Wesley.

Carnegie Task Force on Teaching as a Profession (1986) *A Nation Prepared: Teachers for the 21st Century*, New York: Carnegie Forum on Education and the Economy.

Cave, R. G. (1970) *Partnership for Change: Parents and Schools*, London: Ward Lock.

CIPFA (1988) *Performance Indicators in Schools*, London: Routledge.

Clune, W. H. and White, P. A. (1987) *School-based Management: Institutional Variation, Implementation, and Issues for Further Research*, Madison, WI: Center for Policy Research in Education.

Cohen, L. and Manion, L. (1994) *Research Methods in Education*, 4th edn, London: Routledge.

Conley, D. T. (1991) 'Restructuring schools: educators adapt to a changing world', *Trends and Issues* (6).

Conley, D. T. (1993) 'Roadmap to restructuring: policies, practices and the emerging vision of schooling', Oregon: ERIC (Clearinghouse on Educational Management).

Corbett, H. D. (1990) 'On the meaning of restructuring', *Research for Better Schools*, Philadelphia, PA: ERIC.

Corbett, H. D. (1991) 'Restructuring schools: towards a definition', in Kershner and Connolly (eds) (1991).

Corrick, M. (1996) 'Effective governing bodies, effective schools?', in Earley *et al.* (eds) (1996).

Cox, C. B. and Dyson, A. E. (1969) *Black Paper No. 1: Fight for Education*, London: Critical Quarterly Society.

Craft, A. (1996) *Continuing Professional Development*, London: Routledge.

Creemers, B. (1994) *The Effective Classroom*, London: Cassell.

Creemers, B. (1996) 'The school effectiveness knowledge base', in Reynolds *et al.* (eds) (1996).

Cuban, L. (1988) 'A fundamental puzzle of school reform', *Phi Delta Kappan* 69(5): 341–4.

Darling-Hammond, L. (1996) 'The quiet revolution: rethinking teacher development', *Educational Leadership* 53(6): 4–10.

David, J. L. (1990) 'Restructuring in progress: lessons from pioneering districts' in Elmore *et al.* (1990).

Davies, B. and Anderson, L. (1992) *Opting for Self-Management: the Early Experiences of Grant-Maintained Schools*, London: Routledge.

Day, C. (1990) *Insights into Teachers' Thinking and Practice*, Sussex: Falmer.

Dennison, W. F. and Shenton, K. (1987) *Challenges in Education Management: Principles into Practice*, London: Croom Helm.

DES (1965) *Circular 10/65*, London: HMSO.

DES (1977) *Ten Good Schools*, London: HMSO.

DES (1983a) *Teaching Quality*, London: HMSO.

DES (1983b) *Circular 3/83*, London: HMSO.

DES (1985) *Better Schools*, London: HMSO.

DES (1986a) *Education (No. 2) Act*, London: HMSO.

DES (1986b) *A New Choice of School*, London: DES.

DES (1988) *Education Reform Act*, London: HMSO.

DES (1992) *Education Act*, London: HMSO.

DfE (1993) *Circular 7/93*, London: HMSO.

DfE (1995) *Governing Bodies and Effective Schools*, London: DfE.

Dimmock, C. (ed.) (1993) *School-based Management and School Effectiveness*, London: Routledge.

Drexler, K. E. (1986) *Engines of Creation: the Coming Era of Nanotechnology*, New York: Doubleday.

Drucker, P. F. (1970) *The Effective Executive*, London: Pan Books.

Drucker, P. F. (1974) *Management Tasks, Responsibilities, Practices*, London: Heinemann.

Dudley LEA (1991) *National GRASP Conference*, Dudley: Dudley LEA.

Dunham, J. (1992) *Stress in Teaching*, London: Routledge.

Dunham, J. (1995) *Developing Effective School Management*, London: Routledge.

Earley, P. (ed.) (1988) *Governors' Reports and Annual Parents' Meetings: the 1988 Education Act and Beyond*, Slough: NFER.

Earley, P. (1992) 'Using competences for school management development', *British Journal of In-Service Management* 18(2).

Earley, P. (1993) 'Improving management performance: can competence-based approaches help?', in Green (1993).

Earley, P. (1994) *School Governing Bodies: Making Progress?*, Slough: NFER.

Earley, P. (1996) 'School improvement and OFSTED inspection: the research evidence', in Earley *et al.* (eds) (1996).

Earley, P., Fidler, B. and Ouston, J. (eds) (1996) *Improvement through Inspection?*, London: David Fulton.

Elliott, J., Bridges, D., Ebbutt, D., Gibson, R. and Nias, J. (eds) (1981) *School Accountability*, London: Grant McIntyre.

Elmore, R. F. *et al.* (1990) *Restructuring Schools: the Next Generation of Educational Reform*, San Francisco, CA: Jossey-Bass.

Etzioni, A. (1964) *Modern Organisations*, Englewood Cliffs, NJ: Prentice-Hall.

Everard, K. B. and Marsden, C. (1985) 'Industry's contribution to school management training: a matter of mutual interest', *BACIE Journal* 40(2): 49–52.

Fey, S. (1991) *CTC Characteristics: a Discussion Document*, London: CTC Trust.

Fidler, B. (1996) *Strategic Planning for School Improvement*, London: Pitman.

Fiedler, F. (1967) *A Theory of Leadership Effectiveness*, New York: McGraw-Hill.

Fullan, M. (1985) 'Change processes and strategies at the local level', *The Elementary School Journal* 85 (3): 391–421.

Fullan, M. (1992) 'Visions that blind', *Educational Leadership* 49(5): 20.

Fullan, M. and Hargreaves, A. (1992) *What's Worth Fighting For in Your School?*, Buckingham: Open University Press.

Fullan, M. and Miles, M. (1992) 'Getting reform right: what works and what doesn't', *Phi Delta Kappan* 73(10): 744–52.

Gardner, H. (1983) *Frames of Mind: the Theory of Multiple Intelligences*, New York: Basic Books.

Gardner, H. and Hatch, T. (1989) 'Multiple intelligences go to school: educational implications of the theory of multiple intelligences', *Educational Researcher* 18(8).

Gardner, J. W. (1990) *On Leadership*, New York: The Free Press.

Glatter, R. (ed.) (1989) *Educational Institutions and Their Environments: Managing the Boundaries*, Milton Keynes: Open University Press.

Green, H. (ed.) (1993) *The School Management Handbook*, London: Kogan Page.

Greenfield, J. B. 'Theory about organisations: a new perspective and its implications for schools', in M. Hughes (ed.) (1975) *Administering Education – International Challenge*, London: Athlone Press.

Gretton, J. and Jackson, M. (1976) *William Tyndale: Collapse of a School – or a System?* London: George Allen & Unwin.

Hall, G. E., Wallace, R. C. and Dossett, W. A. (eds) (1973) *A Developmental Conceptualization of the Adoption Process within Educational Institutions*, Austin: RDTCE, University of Texas at Austin.

Halsey, P. 'Implications for school improvement in the United Kingdom', in Hopkins (ed.) (1987).

Handy, C. (1984a) 'Educating for management outside business', in S. Goodlad, (ed.) (1984) *Education for the Professions*, Guildford: SRHE and NFER-Nelson.

Handy, C. (1984b) *Taken for Granted? Understanding Schools and Organisations*, London: Longman.

Handy, C. (1985) *Understanding Organisations*, Harmondsworth: Penguin.

Handy, C. (1989) 'Cultural forces in schools', in Glatter (1989).

Hellawell, D. (ed.) (1984) *Headteachers and Change in Schools in Western Europe*, Brussels: Association for Teacher Education in Europe.

Hersey, P. and Blanchard, K. (1982) *Management of Organizational Behavior: Utilising Human Resources* (4th edn), Englewood Cliffs, NJ: Prentice-Hall.

HMI (1985) *Quality in Schools: Evaluation and Appraisal*, London: HMSO.

HMSO (1956) *The Burnham Report*, London: HMSO.

HMSO (1989) *Schoolteacher Appraisal: a National Framework*, London: HMSO.

Holly, P. and Southworth, G. (1989) *The Developing School*, Lewes: Falmer.

Holmes, B. and McLean, M. (1989) *The Curriculum: a Comparative Perspective*, London: Unwin Hyman.

Holmes Group (1986) *Tomorrow's Teachers,* East Lansing, MI: Holmes Group.

Hopes, C. (ed.) (1986) *The School Leader and School Improvement: Case Studies from Ten OECD Countries*, Leuven, Belgium: Acco.

Hopkins, D. (ed.) (1987) *Improving the Quality of Schooling*, Lewes: Falmer.

Hopkins, D. (1990) 'The international school improvement project (ISIP) and effective schooling: towards a synthesis', *School Organisation* 10(3): 195–202.

Hopkins, D., Ainscow, M. and West, M. (eds) (1994) *School Improvement in an Era of Change*, London: Cassell.

Hopkins, D. and Lagerweij, N. (1996) in Reynolds, D. *et al.* (eds) (1996).

Hord, S. (1987) *Evaluating Educational Innovation*, London: Croom Helm.

Hord, S. (1992) *Facilitative Leadership: the Imperative for Change*, Austin, TX: Southwest Educational Development Laboratory.

Hord, S. (1996) *Communities of Continuous Inquiry and Improvement*, Austin, TX: Southwest Educational Development Laboratory.

Hord, S. and Poster, C. (1993) 'Restructuring schools: lessons from school leaders', in Dimmock (ed.) (1993).

Hoy, W. K. and Miskel, C. G. 'Schools and their external environments' in Glatter (ed.) (1989).

Hoyle, E. (1976) 'Barr Greenfield and organisation theory', *Education Administration* 5(1): 4–6.

Hughes, M. G. 'The professional-as-administrator: the case of the secondary school head', in Peters (ed.) (1976).

Hughes, M. G., Carter, J. and Fidler, B. (eds) (1982) *Professional Development Provision for Senior Staff in Schools and Colleges*, Birmingham: University of Birmingham.

Hutton, W. (1995) *The State We're In*, London: Jonathan Cape.

Isaacson, N. and Bamburg, J. (1992) 'Can schools become learning organisations?', *Educational Leadership* 50(3): 42–4.

Jones, J. (1988) *Evaluation of the Dudley GRASP Project*, London: Janet Jones Associates.

Kershner, K. A. and Connolly, J. A. (1991) *At-risk Students and School Restructuring*, Philadelphia, PA: Research for Better Schools.

Knight, B. (1989) *Managing School Time*, Harlow: Longman.

Koppich, J. E. and Guthrie, J. W. (1993) 'Examining contemporary education-reform efforts in the United States', in Beare and Lowe Boyd (eds).

Lawton, D. and Gordon, P. (1987) *HMI*, London: Routledge.

Leithwood, K. A. (1992) 'The move towards transformational leadership', *Educational Leadership* 49(5): 8–12.

Likert, R. (1961) *New Patterns of Management*, London: McGraw-Hill.

Louis, K. S. and Loucks-Horsley (eds) (1989) *Supporting School Improvement: a Comparative Perspective*, Leuven, Belgium: Acco.

McGregor, D. G. (1960) *The Human Side of Enterprise*, London: McGraw-Hill.

MacGregor, J. (1990) Speech to the North of England Education Conference, *TES* 12 January.

McLaughlin, M. (1990) 'The Rand Change Agent Study revisited: macro perspectives, micro realities', *Educational Researcher* 19(9): 11–16.

Maychell, K. and Keys, W. (1993) *Under Inspection: LEA Evaluation and Monitoring*, Slough: NFER.

Merton, R. K. and Kendall, P. L. (1946) 'The focused interview', *American Journal of Sociology* 51: 541–57.

Miles, M. B. and Ekholm, M. (1991) 'Will new structures stay restructured?', paper presented at the AERA Conference, Chicago, April 1991.

Miles, M. B., Ekholm, M. and Vandenberghe, R. (eds) (1987) *Lasting School Improvement: Exploring the Process of Institutionalisation*, Leuven, Belgium: Acco.

Moon, C. and Ruel, N. (1988) *Individualised Reading,* Reading: School of Education, University of Reading.

Mortimore, P., Sammons, P., Stoll, L., Lewis, D. and Ecob, R. (eds) (1988) *School Matters: the Junior Years,* Wells: Open Books.

Mortimore, P. (1993) *School Effectiveness and the Management of Effective Teaching and Learning,* International Congress for School Effectiveness, Sweden: Norrkoping.

Munn, P. (ed.) (1993) *Parents and Schools: Customers, Managers or Partners?,* London: Routledge.

Murphy, J. (1991) *Restructuring Schools: Capturing and Assessing the Phenomena,* New York: Teachers' College Press.

Murray White, W. (1974) 'Courses for management', *Secondary Education,* June.

Musgrave, P. W. (1968) *The School as an Organisation,* London: Macmillan.

NASSP (1982) *The Effective Principal: a Research Summary,* Reston, VA: National Association of Secondary School Principals.

National Commission on Education (1993) *Learning to Succeed,* London: Heinemann.

National Commission on Education (1996) *Success Against the Odds,* London: Routledge.

National Governors' Association (1986) *Time for Results: the Governors' Report on Education,* Washington, DC: National Governors' Association.

Newman, J. (1985) *Staff Appraisal Schemes in the South Midlands and the South West,* York: Centre for the Study of Comprehensive Schools.

Newsom Report (1963) *Half Our Future,* London: HMSO.

Nias, J. (1980) 'Leadership styles and job satisfaction in primary schools', in Bush, T. *et al.* (eds.) (1980) *Approaches to School Management,* London: Harper & Row.

Nicholson, B. (1997) in *Guardian,* 3 January.

OECD (1989) *Decentralisation and School Improvement,* Paris: OECD–CERI.

OFSTED (1993) *The Handbook for the Inspection of Schools,* London: HMSO.

OFSTED (1995) *Framework for the Inspection of Schools,* London: HMSO.

Ouchi, W. G. (1981) *Theory Z,* Reading, MA: Addison-Wesley.

Ouston, J., Fidler, B. and Earley, P. (eds) (1996) *OFSTED Inspection: the Early Experience,* London: David Fulton.

Page, J. (1990) *An Introduction to High Scope,* Mimeograph, Lane Head Nursery, Walsall.

Percival, W. (1968) 'The head and the problem of size', in Allen (ed.) (1968).

Peters, R. S. (ed.) (1976) *The Role of the Head,* London: Routledge and Kegan Paul.

Plowden Report (1967) *Children and Their Primary Schools,* London: HMSO.

Poster, C. (1976) *School Decision Making,* London: Heinemann.

Poster, C. and Poster, D. (1993) *Teacher Appraisal: Training and Implementation,* London: Routledge.

Purkey, S. C. and Smith, M. S. (1983) 'Effective schools: a review', *The Elementary School Journal* 4: 427–52.

Purkey, S. C., Rutter, R. A. and Newman, F. M. (1987) 'US high school improvement programs: a profile from the *High School and Beyond Supplement* survey', *Metropolitan Education* 1986–87 (Winter): 59–91.

Purkey, W. W. and Novak, J. (1990) *Inviting School Success,* Belmont, CA: Wadsworth.

Raywid, M. A. (1990a) 'The evolving effort to improve schools: pseudo-reform, incremental reform, and restructuring', *Phi Delta Kappan* 72(2).

Raywid, M. A. (1990b) 'The evolving effort to improve schools,' in Elmore *et al.* (1990).

Reavis, C. and Griffith, H. (1992) *Restructuring Schools: Theory and Practice*, Lancaster, PA: Technomic Publishing.

Rée, H. (1968) 'The changed role of the head', in Allen (ed.) (1968).

Report to the Legislature on the Schools for the 21st Century Program (1993), Washington State Board of Education.

Reynolds, D., Creemers, B., Bollen, R., Hopkins, D., Stoll, L. and Lagerweij, N. (eds) (1996) *Making Good Schools: Linking School Effectiveness and School Improvement*, London: Routledge.

Rhoden, C. (1997) 'The self-monitoring school', in White and Poster (eds.) (1997).

Ribbens, P. (ed.) (1997) *Leaders and Leadership in the School, College and University*, London: Cassell.

Rudduck, J. (1981) *Making the Most of the Short In-service Course*, London: Methuen.

Rutter, M., Maughan, B., Mortimore, P. and Ouston, J. with Smith, A. (eds) (1979) *Fifteen Thousand Hours*, London: Open Books.

Sallis, J. (1988) *Schools, Parents and Governors: a New Approach to Accountability,* London: Routledge.

Sashkin, M. and Egermeier, J. (1992) *School Change Models and Processes: a Review and Synthesis of Research and Practice*, Washington, DC: US Department of Education.

Scheerens, J. (1992) *Effective Schooling: Research, Theory and Practice*, London: Cassell.

Schein, E. (1985) *Organisation, Culture and Leadership: a Dynamic View*, San Francisco, CA: Jossey-Bass.

School Management Task Force (1990) *Report to the Department for Education*, London: HMSO.

Stoll, L. and Fink, D. (1996) *Changing Our Schools*, Buckingham: Open University Press.

Suffolk LEA (1985) *Those Having Torches*, Suffolk LEA.

Tannenbaum, R. and Schmidt, W. H. (1958) 'How to choose a leadership pattern', *Harvard Business Review* 366(2): 95–101.

Tannenbaum, R. and Schmidt, W. H. (1973), 'How to choose a leadership pattern', *Harvard Business Review* May–June: 366(2) 162–79.

Taylor Report (1977) *A New Partnership for Our Schools*, London: HMSO.

Thomas, H. and Martin, J. (1996) *Managing Resources for School Improvement*, London: Routledge.

Townsend, T. (ed.) (1997) *Restructuring and Quality: Issues for Tomorrow's Schools*, London: Routledge.

Tuckman, B. W. (1972) *Conducting Educational Research*, New York: Harcourt Brace Jovanovich.

Turner, G. and Clift, P. (1985) *A First Review and Register of School and College Based Teacher Appraisal Schemes*, Milton Keynes: Open University Press.

US Department of Education (1991) 'Developing leaders for restructuring schools: new habits of mind and heart', Washington, DC: Office of Educational Research and Development.

van den Berg, R. M. 'The Concerns-based Adoption Model in the Netherlands and Flanders: state of the art and perspective', in Bollen (ed.) (1993).

van den Berg, R. M. and Vanderberghe, R. (eds) (1986) *Strategies for Large-scale Change in Education: Dilemmas and Solutions*, Leuven, Belgium: Acco.

van den Berg, R. M., Hameyer, U. and Stokking, K. (eds) (1989) *Dissemination Reconsidered: the Demands of Implementation*, Leuven, Belgium: Acco.

van den Hoven, G. (1996) Foreword to Reynolds *et al*. (eds) (1996).

van Velzen, W., Miles, M., Ekholm, M., Hameyer, U. and Robin, D. (eds) (1985) *Making School Improvement Work*, Leuven, Belgium: Acco.

Vroom, V. H. and Deci, E. L. (1970) *Management and Motivation*, Harmondsworth: Penguin.

Watts, G. D. and Castle, S. (1993) 'The time dilemma in school restructuring', *Phi Delta Kappan* 75(3): 306–10.

Weick, K. E. (1976) 'Educational organisations as loosely coupled systems', *Administrative Science Quarterly* 21: 1–19.

West-Burnham, J. (1992) *Managing Quality in Schools*, London: Longman.

West-Burnham, J. (1993) 'Quality assurance in schools', in Green (ed.) (1993).

White, P. (1993) 'Quality in a public service: education', paper delivered at The Teacher as Manager Conference, Institute of Quality Assurance.

White, P. and Poster, C. (eds.) (1997) *The Self-Monitoring School*, London: Routledge.

Whitty, G., Edwards, T., and Gewirtz, S. (eds) (1993) *Specialisation and Choice in Urban Education: the City Technology College Experiment*, London: Routledge.

Williams, M. (1992) 'The achieving school', *Managing Service Quality*, November 1992, Bedford: IFS Publications.

Wilson, E. K. (1971) *Sociology: Rules, Roles and Relationships*, Homewood, IL: Dorsey.

INDEX

Page numbers in *italics* refer to figures and tables.